DEDICATION

To Graham and Julia

I WALK INTO THE OFFICE OF THE HEAD OF THE DISCOVERY CHANNEL AND ASK HIM TO TRUST ME WITH THE INTEGRITY OF THE NETWORK, DEMANDING HE GIVE ME A MILLION DOLLARS AND SIX HOURS OF PRIMETIME PROGRAMMING

SEVEN-FOOT-FOUR ANDRE THE GIANT STARES DOWN AT ME WITH BLOODSHOT EYES, HIS ENORMOUS HEAD INCHES FROM MY FACE AS THOUSANDS CHEER FOR HIM TO TEAR ME APART

SENATOR TED KENNEDY HITS ME THEN RECOILS IN HORROR, BELIEVING I AM THE ASSASSIN HE HAS FEARED FOR YEARS

AS THOUSANDS OF PEOPLE BEG HIM TO RETURN TO THE STAGE, MICK FLEETWOOD JUST LAUGHS AND HANDS ME A COLD BEER

THAT MORNING I SELECTED MY MOST STURDY CLOTHES, CONVINCED I'D BE SPENDING A VERY LONG TIME IN A GREEK PRISON

INS & OUTS - A LIFE IN TELEVISION

1

RAVELLO, ITALY. SUMMER 1992.

I am sitting on a white leather couch across from Gore Vidal. Vidal is wearing a pale pink terry cloth bathrobe and we each are drinking a cold beer. Across a round coffee table strewn with newspapers and books sits the celebrated author of twenty five novels, twenty six nonfiction works, fourteen screenplays and eight stage plays. His face shows some age but remains strong as if his powerful features were a mask. He gestures wildly as he speaks, his beefy hand tightly gripping the sweaty beer can. He has a powerful gaze and his bloodshot eyes light up as he regales me with tales of celebrities.

"Last week Marty sat right there, Marty Scorsese sat where you are, and we were talking about the animal, Oliver Stone. We call him the animal, you know. He was a protégé of Marty's and he's a beast. And earlier last week Peter O'Toole stood right in the doorway behind me and laughed that magnificent laugh of his."

I look past the animated man in the bathrobe at the empty doorway and imagine Peter O'Toole's famous grin doubling over in laughter. Just to the left is a fireplace with a large mantel lined with photographs showing Vidal posing with famous people. These photos were not just of celebrities but of some of the biggest and most elusive names of the twentieth century. People like John F. Kennedy and Paul Newman. What the hell am I doing here?

***

I left my home in Baltimore, USA to write this book in Berlin because Berlin is simply the coolest place I know. Not places like the Reichstag or Checkpoint Charlie with their bad mojo - but the nuances of the Mitte neighborhood.

Graffiti in the Mitte.

After the fall of the Berlin Wall artists flooded into East Berlin for the old buildings and cheap rent, opening shops, boutiques and coffeehouses. Its currently the only European capital where you can still live on a reasonable budget. As the New York Times said recently, "bohemian young people are moving to the city from every part of the globe." The neighborhood I'm staying in is slowly becoming gentrified as graffiti-strewn walls give way to posh boutiques, but it still has a good vibe. If there are cops I haven't seen them. And it is full of young people. Parties spill out onto the streets. It feels like what Greenwich Village could have felt like in the early sixties. I love it.

Trying to organize the book.

I am a television producer. As a teen I sat on my parents' couch watching TV and dreaming dreams, deciding that one day I wanted to make a documentary. I was the youngest of three and no one in my family had even gone to college much less aspired to work in TV. I had no experience. My parents were an upholsterer and a telephone operator.

***

By the time I sat on Vidal's couch I was in my early thirties with experience in every phase of the television business - yet to break into the big time. Weeks earlier, my wife Kim and I were planning a simple vacation to Italy. I read about the region and thought the tragic story of Amalfi and the tsunami that wiped out most of the city in the year 1343 might be a good story for me to develop as a documentary. After a little research I also learned that Gore Vidal and the artist Cy Twombly both lived on the Amalfi Coast. Trying to secure a big name to attach to my project, I wrote to both of their publicists. I had no money, no connections and no deal with a network. I just had an idea. Twombly, a notorious recluse, never responded but I did hear back from Vidal's publisher. Vidal had recently narrated a documentary on the history of Venice and the great man would be happy to meet with me at his home in Ravello. The publicist gave me Gore Vidal's personal telephone number and told me to call when I reached the town's main square.

Kim and I drove down the torturous coastal road from Amalfi to the hill town of Ravello and when we arrived in the square I up dialed the number. A man answered with, "Pronto?" I asked to speak to Gore Vidal and he said, "That's me." He was expecting my call, happy to hear from me, and offered directions to his home but cautioned that I be careful not to pass his gate as the path would lead me straight down the mountain. We set off in search of the gate, missed it and walked halfway down the mountain before heading back up. Finding

9

the elusive gate, we walked through as instructed, across a manicured lawn and suddenly there was La Rondinaia, Vidal's spectacular villa, an architectural treasure that defied gravity by clinging to a cliff on Italy's majestic Amalfi Coast.

Gore Vidal's Ravello home "La Rondinaia".

Red bougainvillea spilled down the whitewashed sides of the home set into the side of a mountain. As I crossed the balcony I could see the azure Mediterranean Sea splash the rocks far below.

And there was Gore Vidal, standing next to the arched front door, bathed in sunlight, dressed in a bathrobe. Who greets guests in a bathrobe? At the time I thought he was just a bit eccentric.

The result was that Gore Vidal looked as disheveled as his home. Books and magazines covered every flat surface in haphazard stacks. But he offered us both a beer and then another and then a third as the three of us happily sat and talked and drank and laughed our asses off.

Only recently I finally learned why he was wearing the robe. Vidal was always cold, a remnant of the hypothermia he'd suffered while serving in the Army in World War II.

Squeezed in between Vidal's fascinating stories and his seemingly endless list of famous friends I did manage to discuss my idea. I never made that documentary about Amalfi. And I never saw Gore Vidal again. In 2012 he died at his home in the Hollywood Hills section of Los Angeles, where he moved in 2003 after selling La Rondinaia for a reported $17 million dollars. I believe he agreed to meet with me that day in 1992 not because he thought my documentary idea was good but because he was simply lonely up there on a cliff, left only with his memories, far from his friends.

***

I'm alone now, far from my own friends. I do have one friend here in Berlin, although we haven't actually met.

Back home while I was planning my trip I was surfing CraigsList Berlin, not sure what I was looking for. Eeva had placed an ad there, a desperate plea for work. The ad was written with care and as I read it I felt something genuine. I responded with sympathy for I had no paying job to offer her.

She is a thirty-four-year-old concert pianist who relocated from Scandinavia in search of employment. I wrote that I was a filmmaker and if she had the time perhaps we could collaborate on a short film while I was in town.

Eeva accepted my offer with the caveat that if real work came her way she would have to take it instead. I friended her on Facebook and she invited me to a recital. I just took the U-Bahn out of East Berlin and far into the West, near the end of the U8 line.

I'm walking a few blocks through a residential neighborhood while a soft snow falls. Its dark and the cobblestone sidewalk is slippery. I do not want to fall and hurt myself, all alone, far from home. Eventually I find St George's Church where the recital is to take place.

I see an old couple pull the heavy wooden door and step from the dark into the light. Then I pause and wonder what I am doing. I really don't know Eeva or anyone else here. I don't want to be seen as a creepy old man stalking a young woman from the internet.

But I take a deep breath and look up at the sky. Silent snow dances in the night air around a street lamp. The cold air reaches deep into my lungs, wakens me and I feel everything will be alright, so I pull the heavy ornate handle and step into the narthex.

Taking a seat in the middle of the church I read about the building. I learn that the church was built in the British sector of West Berlin and served the British military. The pews still bear military badges from each British regiment that served here in post-war Berlin.

Soon Eeva comes out from the sacristy, takes a seat at the piano and plays brilliantly with a program including Ravel, Debussy and Faure. At the reception afterwards, I feel awkward, but I muster up the courage to introduce myself. She is as kind and gracious as I'd hoped. We agree to meet again later in the week for a drink.

I took a chance contacting a stranger in a strange city. I really had no idea who Eeva was. She must have had even greater reservations about me. But we both took that chance.

Travelling alone provides a much greater opportunity to meet people than traveling with others. On a bitter cold night in Switzerland I met four women in a pub who took me under their wings, driving me to the old town in a red convertible, ending the evening laughing while teaching me the Swiss kiss.

My heart leaps when I think of the lovely brunette Italian girl I met on a train through the French Alps and how we couldn't communicate so we just kissed all the way to Italy in a secluded club car.

I always grin when I think of Devlin, the unemployed philosopher I drank with in Dublin, sitting on spent beer kegs in the courtyard of O'Donoghue's Pub while we talked about life and sang with the band.

And the belly laughs I had with those American baseball players from Nettuno I drank with all night on a hot summer night in Rome while we played tricks on the mean waiter at the outdoor cafe near the train station.

All people I met because I was travelling alone. All those good times came flooding back. Those were really good memories of mine where traveling alone led to fun and adventure.

So, I was glad I took that chance and stepped into the recital.

On my walk back to the U-Bahn station after the reception I act like a kid by opening my mouth, so the falling snow can land on my tongue. And I smile a big smile.

All the way back to my neighborhood I am smiling. During that train ride back to the East I begin to recall opening other big doors, ones that eventually led to my unlikely career in television.

It was a wild ride.

Now begins the tale.

Part One

Scratching and Clawing: Beginning a Life in Television

I spent my first week in television with one hand flat, the other one cold.

My first crew responsibility was as a grip. The term 'grip' stems from the need for someone to hold something, as in, "Hey kid. Hold this light stand so it doesn't blow over and kill somebody."

Grips often hold a reflector or a prop or whatever the hell they're told to, often for hours. My big break was I was asked to hold an ashtray and a beer just off screen for an actor.

That was how I spent my first week in the television business: one hand flat, the other hand cold.

Fuck, holding someone else's ashtray is filthy and demeaning. The crew constantly poked fun at me, handing me an ashtray during lunch or while having beers at the local pub. I just grinned.

I knew that if I could hold out I'd be rewarded with learning from these assholes all around me and the mysteries surrounding television production would slowly fade away. And one day I would fuck them back.

And I did.

Our resident star for the week was Forrest Tucker or 'Tuck' as he preferred to be called. Tucker had starred on Broadway and in nearly a hundred Hollywood films but was known to America for his role in the God-awfully-stupid television comedy series *F-Troop*.

We spent a week together shooting TV commercials for a chain of furniture stores. Each morning as Tuck smoothed his grey hair, donned his double-breasted suit and winked into the camera, I stood a few feet away with a Heineken and an ashtray.

Sure, it was a small job but as it turned out a significant one as Tuck chain-smoked cigarettes and averaged six Heinekens each morning before lunch, then another six in the afternoon. Dude could pound some brew.

One quirk about Tuck was the fact that, unlike most other male actors, he refused to wear make-up of any kind. Knowing this the crew decided to make a fool of me, the unknowing grip, by telling me to apply a little powder on him one morning.

I approached him and moved in to apply the powder as I was told. Tuck told me to stop. Thinking he was kidding and believing in the direction I'd been given by the assholes behind me I continued to move in with the powder only to hear Tucker growl and bark at me, drawing muffled chuckles from the amused crew.

Again, I was the butt of the joke, but I swallowed my pride yet again and took it as another lesson learned. If you want to last in this kind of business, you need to develop what I call "rhino skin." Just let it bounce off while fantasizing silently about letting go of the light stand when a certain asshole is under it.

That week I learned how to light for green screen, how to write copy, how to host talent in a studio, how to structure a shoot day and how a crew interacts.

Pretty good for holding my tongue while holding that damn ashtray.

We did have a lot of laughs that week because the crew had a good sense of humor. And not everyone was a dick. Some were downright nice to me.

I also learned that, if you didn't approach him with powder, Forrest Tucker was a pretty cool guy.

It was late June and when I told him it was my mom's birthday he sang Happy Birthday to her over the phone. He also invited the entire crew to visit him on his ranch if we ever got to Texas.

We and heard many stories from his days in Hollywood. Tuck had been linked to a series of steamy affairs with various female movie stars and the story spreading around the crew was that Forrest Tucker was unusually well hung.

The scriptwriter on this shoot was a local wit named David DeBoy and when it came time for Tuck to read a series of tag lines like "See you on the tenth," and "Only this Saturday," David slipped in the line, "Would you like to see my cock?" which Tucker smoothly delivered to howls of laughter from the crew.

With perfect comedic timing, Tuck paused, then followed with, "Do you have two people to help me lift it?"

Soon a slew of bawdy Hollywood stories followed. I stood there laughing, with my left hand wrapped around a Heineken, my right hand holding an ashtray, soaking it all up.

I was an insider - even if I was just one step above a human end table.

Six years after we shot those commercials the cigarettes caught up with Forrest Tucker. He died from lung cancer and emphysema. Those lighthearted furniture spots laced with stories of Hollywood would later prove to be one of the most invaluable paid educational moments of my career.

The Human End Table awaits behind Tuck.

On the set with Forrest Tucker (center) flanked by Billy Ezell on the left, Steve Cook (AKA Dzl) and me on the right. Dzl pulled me into the photo at the last minute. I'm wearing a Houston Astros baseball cap with a WCVT button covering the logo. For me it was a rare moment that week without an ashtray in my hand. I treasure this photo because it's the only one I have of Billy. Billy was a very cool guy and took the time to teach me lighting techniques that I used the rest of my career. Unfortunately, Billy died of AIDS not too long after this photo was taken during the early days of the disease. But I never forgot his kindness. He inspired me to be patient with young people just starting out.

***

In Berlin I'm meeting Eeva at a pub in my neighborhood. I arrive early and look around for her. The bar is full of people, most with laptops sucking up the free Wi-Fi. I sit at the bar and wait. Moments later she arrives. She has a warm smile and we embrace like friends, not strangers. We order at the bar then take our drinks upstairs to a quiet table. Eeva sips a glass of red wine and I drink a beer. We exchange details about our lives. I discuss my writing, my children and describe my home. She tells me about her parents, her dreams and her upcoming trip to San Diego. We are two people in a city full of people, each with our own little stories.

After about an hour and a half our glasses are empty and we both feel the need to get back to something. Eeva has a Skype meeting and I must write. Outside, between the pub and the U-Bahn station she asks a passerby to take our photograph. We smile, a frozen moment in time.

Eeva and me.

We stop again near the steps to the U-Bahn. She will take the train and I will walk. We hope to see one another again. She suggests I write my next book in a cabin in Finland by a lake. Sounds nice.

I invite her to stay in my home if she is ever in Baltimore. Then we embrace again, smile, wave and she disappears down into the station.

As I am walking back to my apartment I breathe deeply, elated. I'm not a stranger anymore. I know one person. I have a new friend and

I'm happy. I've come to believe that friendship is wealth.

Back at my apartment I begin to work again, sitting alone on a couch in Berlin. My hands tap the keyboard. These are the same hands that held an ashtray for Forrest Tucker so many years ago.

They are the hands of a man but not like my father's. His hands were rough. My father's hands were strong and calloused, toughened after decades of pulling fabric over wood and springs to make furniture.

***

I learned a lot from my father. Among a great many other things, my father was a real-life wedding crasher. I'm not kidding.

Walter Dugan was born in 1923. I bear his first name as my middle name. The stock market collapsed when he was six. He left school at nine to sell apples, pencils, whatever he could get his hands on. He remembered times when he didn't eat for three days straight.

The Japanese attacked Pearl Harbor on December 7th, 1941 while Dad was a teenager. Like so many others he joined the Navy and, even though he never made it past the third grade, finished at the top of his class in Gunner's Mate School.

He trained in San Diego when the whole city was draped under camouflage. He was assigned to the USS Briarius, a repair ship that worked the South Pacific.

One day a buddy on the ship told him, "Dugan, you've got enough credits to get out of the Navy."

"Really? When?"

"Today, if you want to. Just get to Okinawa and hop on a ship heading home. There'll be a transport pulling alongside this afternoon. Take it if you want to."

With that, Dad left his ship and sailed for home.

Back in Baltimore Dad fell in with some of his old cronies. They had cool names like Chick, Buns and Belsky. Out of the Navy, Dad also reverted to some of his Depression-Era scrambling.

By this time, he'd acquired a nice suit – and he made the most of it. Every weekend, wedding receptions occurred at the Lithuanian and Polish Halls in the neighborhood. In those days people rarely checked to see if you had an invitation so Dad and his friends would simply get dressed up and slip into one of the receptions for free food and beer.

He even adopted a Polish name – Stan Wasilewski – and his friends adopted fake names as well to blend in, all except Belsky, of course, whose Polish connections came in handy.

Soon the wedding reception venues got wise to this roving band of freeloaders and started checking for invitations at the door.

Fortunately, Belsky and his two brothers were of an age that nearly each week at least one of them received a wedding invitation from a Polish friend or relative.

As a bonus, the invitations had multiple documents inside – the announcement, the reception details, the RSVP card, directions, etc. so Belsky would simply distribute parts of the invitation to his friends. One invitation could get in up to five guys.

Once inside the complex, the group would disperse and cruise from one reception to another, offering advice to the others on available menu and bar items. Dad blended in so well that he was once mistaken for one of the Polish Hall officials by a state senator at one of the receptions.

"I really like what you've done with the restoration of the building," the Senator told him. Not missing a beat Dad replied, "Thank you. A lot of money and hard work went into it."

Not his money or hard work.

One of the lessons Dad imparted upon me was that if you didn't know what you were doing at least try and look like you knew what you were doing. That advice would get me far in the television business.

One weekend Dad's luck ran out while wedding-crashing. As he danced with the bride he felt a tap on his shoulder. He spun around to see the father of the bride who said, "Excuse me, but I'd like you and your friend under the table over there to please leave." Pulling a drunken Belsky out from under a nearby table, Dad left and vowed never to sneak back into another wedding. From that point on, the only weddings he attended were the ones he was invited to. But he always cruised through the other rooms to sample the fare.

***

Starbucks vs Café Cinema.

In Berlin, I write through the night until dawn. I sleep until noon then at midday find myself wandering toward Starbucks. Standing in line I look around and feel I could be at any Starbucks in the world. Instead I slip out the door and backtrack into the dark narrow coffee shop next door.

It is cool and dark inside. I expect to see Leonard Cohen brooding in the corner. The few patrons sipping coffee barely look up from their newspapers as I step out of the light and into the darkness. Although a rare winter sun blazes on the street, the long dark passage called Café Cinema is almost pitch dark. Each little table has a tall white candle burning on it.

Candle and latte at Cafe Cinema.

I take off my coat, sit down and order a cappuccino and, sure enough, an old Leonard Cohen song begins to softly play in the background. The dark mellow vibe matches my mood and instantly I feel rewarded for going away from the ordinary.

My mind wanders back to my earliest childhood and the difficulty I used to have making friends. Born late to older parents most of my cousins were around ten years older than me.

My mother didn't like the other kids in the neighborhood much. So, I spent a lot of time alone. I became creative as a reflex of this isolation to entertain myself.

Creativity was a survival technique. I came from humble roots but began to develop big dreams. No one in my family had the kind of grandiose dreams I seemed to have.

No, I was from a family of bootleggers.

***

My mother's side of the family was hardscrabble and adventurous. Her mother - my maternal grandmother - was West Baltimore's most notorious bootlegger.

While Prohibition outlawed the manufacture and distribution of alcoholic beverages in the US from 1920 to 1933, Maryland was the only state never to pass a state enforcement act.

Enforcement of Prohibition was never strong in Baltimore. As a result, Baltimore became known throughout the country as the center for resistance to prohibition.

And right in the middle of it was my grandmother, Minnie Childs.

My bootlegging grandmother Minnie holding my mother, the infant she would soon toss out her second story window while fleeing the law. My Godmother Mary is on the left with her sister Ella on the right.

During prohibition, although the city's breweries and saloons were officially shut down, Minnie had other ideas.

In those days, half the population of the state of Maryland lived in Baltimore – and they were a thirsty bunch of bastards. My grandmother lived in a row house near the corner of Amity and Pratt Streets, a few blocks west of what is now Baltimore's Inner Harbor complex.

She lived in what we now call a townhouse but what everybody back then called a row house. Minnie's was second from the end. Next door, the row house on the end had been converted into a saloon with a bar and about a half dozen bar stools on one side with tables and chairs down the other side.

Minnie made a living tending that bar and hosting second-floor poker games. Upstairs, in her house next door, she made home brew in the bath tub. My mother siphoned beer into bottles as a child.

By all accounts Minnie lived a wild life. She had a parade of colorful characters always coming or going. My grandfather had long since split the scene leaving Minnie to fend for herself and their four children.

Minnie had a boyfriend named Happy, a carefree soul who frequented the bar. One of the regular poker players at the bar was another character named Dutch. Dutch was a bonafied hobo who rode the rails of the B & O Railroad that ambled across the street from the bar.

My mother told me of a time when Dutch showed up on Minnie's doorstep so hungry he could only eat broth for four days until his system became accustomed to real food again. Minnie that nursed him back to health. His shoes had fallen apart and were held together with wire. Minnie found him a new pair. And when Dutch recovered, he took off on the rails again.

Local officials turned a blind eye toward the distribution of liquor and it was left to federal officials to uphold the law. One lazy May Saturday afternoon in 1926, just prior to my mother's birth, the Feds burst into my grandmother's home, confiscated her beer-making equipment and shut down her entire operation. They busted up the bar with an ax and threatened to throw my grandmother in jail if she resumed the manufacture of alcoholic beverages.

They let her off with a warning because she was eight months pregnant.

Minnie may have been pregnant, but she was resourceful. Within days she acquired new beer-making gear, put the bar back together and began production again. She also vowed that the next time the Feds came, she'd be ready for them.

And they did come again, one year later, in force.

The year was 1927, the height of Prohibition in America. It was another sunny Saturday. My Aunt Mary was playing around the corner when she saw men smashing a neighbor's bar with axes. She ran home and told my grandmother the news. Minnie had taken in a lodger in her spare bedroom on the top floor of the row house.

He used to hang out the window to smoke and it was the lodger who first saw the Feds crossing the street, rapidly approaching my grandmother's house. The lodger bolted down the steps shouting, "Here they come, Minnie!"

With that, my grandmother rang a buzzer alerting her friends in the bar to clear out. Men from the bar grabbed whatever they could carry and ran out the back door and down the alley while my grandmother headed for the fire escape. Just then the lodger grabbed Minnie by the arm.

Mom gets dropped from the window while patrons and Minnie flee.

"Wait! What about the baby?" the lodger asked.

My mother was an infant lying in a small crib in the hall. Minnie saw her boyfriend Happy run out of the bar and into the alley. "Hey Hap!" she yelled from the window and pointed to the baby in the lodger's arms.

Happy ran into the small yard behind Minnie's house and positioned himself under the second story window. The lodger leaned out and dropped my infant mother out the second story window and into his waiting arms while Minnie shot up the fire escape and disappeared over the rooftops.

This story was passed down to me as a piece of family lore. I remember my grandmother as an old lady. She was feisty and cursed with abandon. Upon recalling the story of the day, they dropped my mother out of a second story window, we kids would all speculate that Happy had dropped her on her head, thereby explaining why she was as ditsy as she was.

***

I grew up believing that my mother was the real-life character Lucille Ball portrayed in the hit TV series *I Love Lucy*.

One pleasant day during the summer of 1973 my mother was babysitting my sister's two-year-old son when she noticed a pile of laundry waiting to be cleaned.

Determined to help, she marched downstairs to the lower floor with the basket, through the small foyer, past the club room with its bar and pool table and into my brother-in-law's posh in-home office. She placed the spoiled laundry on top of his antique mahogany desk and opened a set of panel doors revealing a washing machine and dryer.

She dumped in the clothes and, without measuring, a generous dollop of laundry detergent. Closing the lid, she couldn't decide whether this load represented a full load or a half load, so she cocked the dial between the two. Happy, she returned upstairs to catch the second half of *The Price is Right*.

Hours later my sister and brother-in-law returned and stood wide-eyed by the front door. They noticed something strange - a surge of soap bubbles pulsating from under the front door. They opened the door and *SPLUGE!* a giant wave of soapy water rushed out the door and down the sidewalk. With the knob cocked between two positions, the washing machine didn't know when to stop filling – so it didn't. Mom flooded my sister's entire first floor with water and soap suds.

The next time Mom was (reluctantly) asked to babysit, she was told not to worry about the laundry.

My sister and brother-in-law were simply going out to dinner. My brother-in-law, a powerful and respected man in the insurance industry, would begin traveling early the next day for a series of very important business meetings out of state and they wanted a peaceful romantic meal alone before his big trip.

Mom was desperate to make up for the laundry debacle, so she scoured the house for something nice she could do. While going to the bathroom she noticed that the steam from the shower had pealed back a few corners of the wallpaper. She began a mission, rooting through every drawer for something to use to repair it. Near the suitcase my brother-in-law had packed for his trip she found the perfect solution: a large roll of double-sided tape.

This time when my sister and brother-in-law returned they were greeted by Mom, standing in the doorway, beaming proudly.

"The wallpaper was peeling off the wall in the bathroom, but I fixed it with double-sided tape. I used up the tape but the wallpaper is all fixed!" she said with a smile.

My brother-in-law turned white.

"Double-sided tape . . ." he gasped. "Where did you find it?"

"Next to your suitcase," she replied.

"Mom, that's the tape I use to hold on my toupee. It's special order. That was the last roll."

My brother-in-law's toupee was so life-like and well-made that few people even knew he wore one. So much for the business trip.

With genetics like this it's little wonder I made a career in the chaotic world of television. My dad's cool tenacity allowed me to open big doors and my mother's clumsy self-assuredness guaranteed I'd stumble right through them.

***

My television career began less than a decade later, in the early eighties, shortly before a new cable network named ESPN was launched. I had great expectations for my career. ESPN, not so much.

"Who's going to watch that?" I remember saying, looking at a large white banner with the letters ESPN in red in the hallway at Flite Three. Since then ESPN has grown to become the worldwide leader in sports programming with eight US television networks, an international presence in 190 countries, a US radio network that reaches 24 million listeners a week and a deep presence online.

Although it is currently struggling a little with competition in the pay-tv industry rising and people trimming back their cable bills, it is still recognized as one of the most successful television ventures of all time.

So much for my ability to predict the future.

I had been weaned on a very limited TV landscape. Growing up in Baltimore there were three major network stations, a couple of small UHF stations that offered mostly reruns, one PBS station and maybe I could pick up a DC station if I put the antenna near the back-bedroom window.

Sports was a topic squeezed into five-minutes during the local news. Five minutes. I thought, "How could they drag that out to 24 hours?"

Nine months after the debut of ESPN, CNN was launched. Again, I didn't see the point. CNN is now a dominant force in the world, a 24-hour news giant seen in over 212 countries and territories, but I didn't see that coming either.

"These networks won't last six months," I scoffed.

Inadvertently, I was poised to benefit from an explosion of TV networks, but I failed to see the future of cable TV at the time.

I missed other opportunities, too - not just in cable but also in syndicated programming.

Syndicated shows are those sold to individual stations in a market. Some examples of syndicated shows are *Ellen*, *Wheel of Fortune* and *The Doctors*.

Oprah Winfrey was a regular at Flite Three in those days. Of course, she wasn't one of the planet's most influential women yet. She hadn't yet broken into the syndicated market. She was simply another local TV personality that would come by to cut radio promos.

Oprah co-hosted a talk show on Baltimore's WJZ called *People are*

Talking along with a nice guy named Richard Sher. In her memoir Oprah recalls her time in Baltimore as a difficult period punctuated by sexism and negative stereotypes but she did spend seven and a half years in my hometown, honing the skills that would eventually help her dominate the world of syndicated daytime television for twenty-five years, making her one of the richest and most successful TV personalities of all time.

She was a warm and friendly person, although, if you can believe it, somewhat shy. At Flite Three she'd sit in the audio booth next to Sher, recording the radio spots that promoted each edition of their program.

They were regular customers, coming in each week with a new series of promos to cut. If I wasn't busy I'd sit in a watch. I remember Oprah was always stifling a laugh as Sher really enjoyed trying to crack her up during those sessions.

Once Sher got Oprah laughing she couldn't stop. He liked to really get her whipped up. They acted like schoolchildren who weren't supposed to laugh, and they would occasionally both totally lose it with uncontrollable laughter. It was the primary reason I liked to sit in on their sessions. I still have an old cassette of their outtakes lying around in a shoebox somewhere.

Oprah left Baltimore and began a journey of unparalleled media success. In fact, I could have been on the ground floor as her producer, gone with her to Chicago and been the darling of the industry – but I didn't.

I did apply to be her producer at WJZ when the job opened. Not because I thought Oprah Winfrey was a genius. Not because I foresaw Oprah's talk show would become the highest rated show of its kind in history. Not because I was smart enough to see a good thing coming. No, I just needed a job and I had some experience producing at the college radio station.

Like an awful lot of jobs, I applied for, I didn't get it. Oh, well. Your loss, baby!

***

Flite Three had been the place that put me on the Forrest Tucker shoot holding an ashtray. Before Flite Three I had spent most of my time developing skills as a radio announcer at my college, Towson State University, north of Baltimore.

I wanted an internship at Flite Three because they did a lot of radio spots, like the Oprah/Sher ones. But they didn't have an internship program. So, I told them, "Look, it's free labor. Just ask someone to give me a grade at the end of the semester. I'll show up every week and work for free. I'll take care of all the paperwork. What do you say?"

Well, they said yes.

I went to Flite Three to learn radio production, but the company was breaking into TV and they kept sending me, the intern, on shoots to lend a hand.

My very first day on the job I met a grizzled veteran director supervising the edit of some political commercials. Two things he said remain with me to this day. The first one was about politics and commercials.

He said, "Kid, you can fool some of the people all of the time. And that's our target audience."

After some of the elections I've witnessed I know he was telling the truth.

His second quote was about the television business in general. "If you want a long career in television, never lose your taste for cheap

33

food."

Damn, he was right about that, too. After thirty-five years in the business, often grabbing a bite whenever I could, he was right about that, too.

Hell, I only spoke to the dude for a minute and he was profound on two points. I wish I could remember his name.

In those days the business of television was expanding rapidly.

I was caught up in the undertow.

Me and blues great Willie Dixon in a shot from this era.

***

Four girls deliberate at the door of a Berlin clothing shop before ducking in and I wander in behind them. The clothes are nothing special, all things I've seen before. Then a pale white t-shirt catches my eye. On it the wrestler Andre the Giant holds a man high above his head. His big ugly face is a familiar one.

Three decades ago Andre the Giant breathed into my face and looked like he wanted to fuck me up.

As a lowly intern, I was asked to do the most menial jobs. Like take the Flite Three van and make a special delivery to The Capital Centre, an 18,000-seat arena on the outskirts of Washington, DC. They had rented a one-inch machine from us. It may sound small, but one inch refers to the width of the tape. The machine was a Sony BVH 2000 – a mainstay in professional television for two decades - but to me it was a four-foot high, one-hundred-and-twenty-pound anvil - heavy as hell and worth eighty thousand bucks - so don't drop it.

My boss had recently destroyed one when he put it in the van and then drove off without securing it down, only to have it fall and smash into pieces. So, I had to be extra careful with this one.

Back in my ashtray-holding days, an engineer would record a sporting event onto the one-inch machine and physically slip the reel-to-reel tapes back and forth with his hands live on the air. This was the first instant replay. It may sound low tech, but it was the first time anyone ever saw a sports play over again, in slow motion, and it was an immediate hit with viewing audiences.

The Capitol Centre was a big-time client since it was the home of *The Washington Bullets* (now *The Wizards*) basketball team and *The Washington Capitals* hockey team. I didn't know why the Cap Centre had rented the machine. All I knew was that I needed to deliver it at a predetermined time. Just drive the damn thing there and don't fuck it up.

I drove the forty-five miles south to Washington from Baltimore but as I turned onto the road leading into the big parking lots of the Capitol Centre I was amazed at all the cars leaving. I thought that the event was cancelled. Nope. Whatever it was, it was so popular that it was sold out and they were turning hundreds of people away.

I pulled the van right up, flashed my paperwork and drove down into the bowels of the arena. Two guys met me and took the heavy one-inch machine safely out of the van. Thankfully my job was done. I was relieved to have made the delivery without incident. Free for a while and not too eager to scoot back to work, I decided to hang around backstage.

I stepped into the control room and saw what amounted to an in-house TV production facility with a wall of monitors. Off to the side a director lazily offered orders to a camera crew in the stands as they interviewed spectators.

"Let's slate him Asshole #1, and the guy in the yellow shirt, he's Asshole #2," the director said.

"What's the event tonight?" I asked.

The director looked at me and smirked.

"Professional wrestling," he replied.

Never having been backstage in an arena before, I asked, "Mind if I hang around?"

"Help yourself," he replied.

The director gave me a laminated pass on a lanyard that read "Full Access." I slipped it around my neck and watched him work. I'd never seen a show directed from a control room before and it fascinated me.

"OK, that's enough of this interview crap. Cue up Asshole #1 and be ready to pull it up when I call for it," sighed the director. He turned to me tiredly and sighed, "I hate wrestling." "Yeah," I thought, "no shit."

As the actual wrestling began things moved more quickly. All the crew wore headsets and the director rapidly called out shots and gave them orders. Each crew member had a specific role. The director called the shots, the technical director pushed the buttons, and the character generator - or CG - operator typed the words that would appear on the screen. The producer sat close by and told the director what was coming up next.

There was also an event expert next to the producer who knew each wrestler and their manager, so each could be identified correctly. The audio guy ran the mixing board, but he sat in a separate room and we could see him through a little glass window.

In yet another room sat an engineer and a tape operator. They were sequestered away from everyone else because the big hot machines they operated generate a lot of noise. The engineer tweaked the cameras remotely, so they had the proper exposure and color correction. The tape operator was responsible for recording the program – and he was the one providing slow motion playback with the one-inch machine.

There is a tension and excitement to a live production that just isn't there during a studio shoot, where you can do things over again if you mess up. With live TV, if you mess up, everyone sees it as it happens. These guys were professionals and even though no one seemed particularly hyped about the wrestling I could feel their adrenaline pumping.

The director did most of the talking and the world of production had a language all its own:

"Ready camera one. Take one. When I get off you, go in for a headshot. Ready five. Start your zoom… dissolve to five. Got a lower third on this guy? Ready two… but let me see it in preview… is the spelling correct? OK, let's cut to two with the key and bring it in… now. Go wide three, with a slow push when I come to you."

I found it all very interesting and exciting.

After a while I stepped out of the Control Room and began to wander around the backstage. This is where things began to go south.

I turned a corner and saw a strange sight and one I'll never forget. Standing there were about a dozen men – all *huge* men – dressed in colorful tights. They were standing in a row with their backs to me, peeping through cracks in a big red velvet curtain. They were all very quiet. Then suddenly the lights came on, the curtains were thrown open and two big sweaty guys also in tights came through the curtains and joined the other men. All the big men in tights cheered and slapped the newcomers on their backs. "What the hell is going on here?" I thought. The group dispersed and joyfully went into a nearby room where they collapsed into chairs around a big table. I crept over and peered down the hall where the curtains were, and I saw the arena in all its glory.

The lights were up and the crowd was milling around. Music played as workers began constructing a large box around the wrestling ring with chain-link fencing. Curious, I walked down the hall to the edge of the ramp leading to the stage. I'd never seen professional wrestling and this was all alien to me. I looked up and saw a dude watching the construction activity and asked him, "What's going on?"

"Cage event," he replied.

"What's that?"

"Biggest thing of the night. First man out of the cage still standing is the winner."

Well, biggest event of the night, huh? Maybe I should stick around and see what all the fuss is about. The place held over 18,000 and the arena was jam-packed with every seat filled, even high up in the rafters. The energy out here was more powerful than anything I'd witnessed in the control room.

I stood there in awe, folded my arms over my full access pass and took it all in. The workers finished building the cage and the crowd began to get restless. Some started to scream while others stomped their feet. Then the lights snapped off plunging the arena into complete darkness. With that, the crowd erupted in a deafening roar. I'd never experienced anything like it. In the darkness I froze in place wondering what would happen next.

Then – BAM – a spotlight came on, seemingly right in my eyes. I turned and squinted as – BAM – a second spotlight came on, totally blinding me. I tried to see but I couldn't because it felt like the lights were right in my eyes. I put my hands up and as I did the crowd roar exploded with a thunderous stomping roar, tripling the intensity.

What the hell did they see? I couldn't see a fucking thing. Slowly my eyes began to adjust and I started to make out the crowd. They were all on their feet, screaming, fists clenched and arms thrust out, leaning forward and looking – at me! What the fuck?! I stood there shocked for a second not knowing what to do.

Then, slowly, I turned around.

Now I saw what they saw.

Right behind me, two inches away stood Andre the Giant, all seven foot, four inches of him. With his legs wide spread, fists set into his waist he peered down at me from above with a wry, twisted smile. Jesus, his enormous head was the size of a damned watermelon. His crazed bloodshot eyes stared into mine from behind a mass of wild black curly hair. Only inches away I could feel his hot breath on my face. I looked at him and he snorted.

It was at that moment I realized I was blocking the entrance of the biggest name on the bill, perhaps the most popular wrestler of all time. I stepped aside, weakly smiled and swept out my arm as if to welcome him to the cage. Not sure what he might do, he thankfully stomped right past me to thunderous applause. When I went back to the control room I got quite a laugh-filled welcome from the amused crew.

Even the director was smiling.

Andre the Giant stares me down while thousands cheer.

Looking at his big fat face on that t-shirt in Berlin made me smile, too. In discussions about the best wrestler ever his name is always in the conversation.

After his death in 1993 Andre the Giant became the very first inductee into the World Wrestling Federation Hall of Fame.

Graffiti depicting the face of Andre the Giant on Torstraße in Berlin.

2

Looking into the mirror in my little rented apartment in Berlin I see a man who has seen many things.

My left ear has some slight hearing loss, a condition suffered by many in my profession. Crew headsets feature only a left ear cup since the right side of a cameraman's head nuzzles up to the camera's eyepiece. If you work in TV long enough eventually a loud blast of feedback will damage your left ear.

I consider my eyes and see the eyes that have seen everything I've experienced. I think of my friend Tony, a career camera operator who developed cancer in his right eye after decades of pressing it up to an eyepiece. Did those years of camerawork give Tony eye cancer? Who knows? I do know that, as a freelancer, Tony had to work up until the day his body broke down. He was admitted into the hospital and that is where he died.

As you age some strange things begins to happen. One of them is your friends begin to die.

It is a fact that the longer you live the more your old friends will, one by one, pass away. What a morbid thought.

But we will all experience it. Unless we are the friend that dies first.

So far, so good.

At father's 90th birthday party only my mother was from his generation. Planning the party, I tried to find old friends of his, even siblings of old friends, but they were all gone.

Friendships are the measure of true wealth. The most impactful friendships develop during times when people have long periods of being together with no agenda. People make deep friendships by hanging out. It is during these times that ideas are discussed, tangents explored and relationships tested.

That is why, as we get older, it is harder to make the kind of deep lasting friendships we made when we were younger. As adults the workplace is often competitive, filled with people thrown together with different backgrounds. Having children of your own makes the process of friend-making even more complicated because all that unstructured free time evaporates.

As we age and further develop our own sense of self we become even pickier, creating lists of requirements for friends (and lovers), quickly dismissing people who don't meet our expectations.

We tend to stay busy and schedule our time, getting together with the few new people we meet for concerts, birthday parties or a sporting events, but we rarely do we just hang out with new people for long periods of time. When we do, at a retreat or on a cruise, we tend to make new friends but even then, it's often not like the deep lasting friendships forged in youth when we literally hung out all the time.

Researchers studying friendship return to three things that are factors in creating great, lasting friendships: proximity, repeated unplanned interactions and an environment that encourages people to let their guard down.

For many, high school or college are the places where this type of friendship-forging tends to occur. The deepest friendships I forged came from hanging out at the college radio station. The people I met there remain some of my closest friends today.

We all thought we wanted to be rock DJs and we all were, for a while.

In the late '70s and early '80s, there was only one place for progressive rock in Baltimore: Towson State University's rock and roll renegade WCVT-FM. I chose to attend Towson primarily because of the cool campus radio station. I loved the place. Run totally by students, this powerhouse cranked out programming twenty-one hours a day and all weekend long. WCVT is gone now, but damn we had great times hanging out there. And the confidence I acquired would serve me well in my television career.

Part of the gang - Stu Foote, musician Joanne Dodds, Jerry Toulos (top hat), Babs Levadahl, Brice Freeman, John Johnson (back to camera), Charlotte Bauernfeld, Kevin Novak (back to camera), Rod Misey (AKA the Plainclothes Punk) and Dave Steplovich.

I was first trained as a DJ on WCVT's AM sister station one night after hours. Brice Freeman was one of the first people I met there and today, thirty-five years later, we are still friends, playing poker once a month. Brice became my mentor. He trained me how to be a DJ and my first day was memorable.

The AM station served only the campus and was off the air for the evening when Brice invited me to learn the ropes. I played a record and when it was over I opened the mike and said, "That was The Beatles from the White Album. Now, here's Brice Freeman with the news." Then I opened the newsroom mike. Brice read some news stories and that was it. Of course, Brice hadn't pre-read the stories; this was just practice for me. As it happened, Brice cracked up over a story about a man who had been in a bizarre accident near the campus. We joked back and forth about it on the open mikes and I played another record. I thought I had done well.

Then the phone rang.

Apparently, unbeknownst to us, you couldn't really turn off the AM station as it was hard-wired to the University Union and the dorms. A young woman called to complain "about that cruel newscaster and the poor man who was injured."

"Congratulations," Brice said. "You're now a DJ."

One of my first shifts was a midnight-to-three slot playing rock on the FM station that went out to all of Baltimore. It was a good shift since many of our listeners were weird night owls. I relieved Kevin Novak who played jazz up to midnight. Since he got off the air so late and the building was already locked I had to let him out and lock the door behind him. When Novak's shift was over and mine began, I put on an Alice Cooper album, one on which the first three songs ran together. I figured I had at least twelve minutes to go downstairs, let Novak out, and lock the door behind him.

Once you're a DJ for a while you get an amazing sense of time. I had twelve whole minutes, so Novak and I stood by the door and talked for a while.

When I returned to the booth, I noticed that the old Alice Cooper album was skipping and it had been skipping on the very first song.

Then the phone rang.

It was Brice. By then Brice had become the Program Director, the boss of the station.

"I was in my car," Brice said, "and I heard the record start to skip. Since I was following my girlfriend in her car I couldn't even pull over to call you. All I could do was count."

"How many skips?" I reluctantly asked.

"Seventy-seven," he replied.

My DJ career was off to a good start.

With that kind of sparkling performance behind me, soon I rose to the rank of FM Operations Director, Brice's right-hand man. One of my most important duties was to fill the weekend All-Night Shows with volunteers. It sounds bad, working midnight to six in the morning for no pay, but usually it wasn't too difficult to get someone to do it. We had about a hundred and twenty students working at the station during its heyday and almost half of them were certified as FM DJ's. But the inevitable did occasionally happen as it did one Saturday night. I couldn't find anyone else and I had to do the show myself.

On this particular Saturday night, I was dog tired. My internship was over at Flite Three but by then they had developed a need for me, so I was working there part-time. I had a regular gig with Metro Traffic Control every weekday. I was also attending school as a full-time student, working at the radio station a lot and doing a lot of dating. By the time the wee hours of Saturday night rolled around I was beat.

I hung in there for the first few hours or so on pure adrenaline but by 4:00 AM I was looking pale and feeling grim. The fluorescent light in the studio bore a hole in my skull as I fought to keep my eyes open. I put on George Harrison's *Apple Jam*, which took up the entire side of an album and laid my head down on the console for a moment. Forty minutes later my eyes cracked open, the glare of the unforgiving fluorescent light blinding me.

Then I heard it. *Wif. Wif. Wif. Wif.*

Apple Jam had run out probably twenty minutes earlier. I was guilty of dead air. Then I laughed. Hell, it was the middle of the night. I opened the mike laughing, "Guess what? I fell asleep. If anyone is out there, you probably fell asleep, too. Wake up and turn off the radio. I'm goin' home..." Then I fumbled around and found the cart that played the sign-off announcement, Jimi Hendrix's version of the National Anthem. Inspired while it played, I got a second wind. So, I followed the sign off announcement with the sign-on announcement, signifying the beginning of a new broadcast day. I lasted another few songs, got winded again and went home around 4:30 in the morning. I'd done my best and that would have to be good enough, Baltimore.

Based on such stellar achievements within a few months I followed in Brice's footsteps and was elected Program Director of the station. I felt I made a lot of good decisions as PD, but if I'm at all smart, I'll never forget one spectacularly stupid decision.

I was driving home from the station through the city one evening when I saw all the big local TV news trucks parked outside of the Baltimore Gas & Electric building.

"I smell a story," I said to the guy I was giving a ride home. "Let's check it out."

We went into the BG&E building only to find some guy being

interviewed across the lobby about forty yards away. We couldn't get anywhere near him. Frustrated I asked a janitor what was going on.

"Nuclear leak," he said.

"Oh my God! A nuclear leak! Where?"

"I think it was Calvert Cliffs (a big nuclear power facility in Maryland)," he said as he shuffled off with his broom.

I turned to my friend.

"I gotta call the radio station. Do you have any money?"

In the days before cell phones a corner pay phone was the only option. He gave me two quarters. That was the beginning of my downfall. If he'd been broke, I'd have saved myself a lot of embarrassment. Even one quarter would have been plenty. But he gave me two. At the time each public phone call cost twenty-five cents. I could make not one but two phone calls.

I raced to a phone booth outside and called the station. Doug Albright was on the air.

"Doug, it's Jeff. You gotta break programming, man. Just cut off the song you're playing and tell the people there's been a nuclear leak. Tell 'em that details are sketchy but you'll have more information during the news."

"What?"

"I don't have time, Doug. Just do it, man!"

"OK, you're the boss."

Now, that was probably bad enough, but no, I still had another quarter.

I slipped the quarter into the slot. "Hello, information? Get me the number to the Associated Press." Calling 411 did not require a charge and the quarter came back out of the phone. The operator gave me the number, and I quickly slipped the coin in again and hastily dialed the number.

"Hello?"

"Yes, this is Jeff Dugan from WCVT. There's been a nuclear leak."

"What?"

"Jeff Dugan, WCVT. There has been a nuclear leak at the Calvert Cliffs Nuclear Plant."

"Who is this?"

I paused then asked, "Is this the Associated Press?"

"No, it is not."

In my haste I had misdialed the number and had inadvertently reached an elderly black woman somewhere in Baltimore City.

Undaunted, with the need to serve my fellow broadcasters (and a desire to get my name on that little sheet of paper that clicked out of the Associated Press machine back at the station), I pressed on.

"Ma'am, please get a pen."

God bless her, the old lady sat down the phone and went off in search of something to write with. She quickly returned.

"Now what is it, young man?"

"You gotta call The Associated Press, ma'am. Tell them Jeff Dugan sent you. There is a nuclear leak. At Calvert Cliffs. This is urgent. Thank you. Goodbye."

I drove home with a feeling of accomplishment. As I strode into the house I tossed down my keys and proudly walked right up to my father and asked him if he'd heard about the leak.

"Oh, yeah," he said. "That was about three days ago. Nothing to it."

The leak being reported on had occurred three days earlier and it had been measured at 1/100th of a millirem, a miniscule amount that posed absolutely no danger to the community. This was a non-story. But I didn't bother to learn the facts before I made those calls.

Ashen-faced, I called Doug Albright back at the radio station.

"I've ripped apart the entire newsroom," Doug gasped, nearly out of breath. "I was looking for something on this leak, anything. Then I found a little item stuck up on the hook about three days old. I led with it. "

"Uhh... Good job," I stammered and hung up the phone.

Fortunately, nothing ever came of my mistake as my friends at the radio station quickly forgot about it. I never knew what happened to the little old lady I accidentally scared half to death, God bless her.

***

Meanwhile, the hours at Flite Three were getting grueling, too. But I was learning television. One gig was memorable. It started with a surgery. Not mine, thank God, but that of an unsuspecting senior citizen.

We'd been hired to document an operation, ostensibly for training purposes, except the only training that could possibly come from this recording was how *not* to do it.

We were shooting in the operating room of a huge hospital in Baltimore. It started out fun as the crew was fitted with surgical garb from head to toe. We were instructed not to touch anything, especially the surgical instruments since they were carefully sanitized.

Unfortunately, within moments of entering the operating room my jacket lightly brushed a table full of surgical tools. The head of the team scowled, her disdain undisguised by her surgical mask. "Replace that tray!" she barked, and two people shoved me aside and clattered away a table full of shiny silver tools, whispering obscenities under their breath. I imagined a team of laborers somewhere spending hours polishing scalpels only to learn that they now had to work through the weekend to make up for a brush from my bulky coat.

After some tense waiting (while I froze in place) a new tray full of shiny tools was wheeled in, followed by the patient.

The subject of our attention was a woman in her late sixties and overweight. She needed a knee replacement and the surgical team got right to work. I should say here that prior to my internship at Flite Three, I might have been a bit squeamish about seeing someone's flesh cut open, but I'd spent countless nights making copies of graphic surgical procedures depicting doctors peeling back faces. By this time, I'd become so desensitized I could've eaten a chili dog while watching them cut open this old lady.

It turned out she had a fake knee already and the old one had to be removed before they could put the new one in. This proved difficult since it looked like the old fake knee was cemented to her leg bone. For the next two hours I watched as the surgeon took everything from a hammer and chisel to a hacksaw to her knee. At one point he put his foot up on the surgical table and just pried it off with a crowbar, screaming, "C'mon you fucker!" The cameras kept on rolling. Finally, the hard-plastic joint chipped off to cheers of relief.

"Fuck that. I need a cigarette," the surgeon said, wiping his brow.

We relaxed and walked away, all except the patient of course, flat on her back, leg splayed open.

One by one, the surgical team shuffled out of the operating room and dispersed. The other TV guys, the surgeon and I slipped down the hall and out a side door to get some fresh air. The cool night was refreshing after the tension inside. The surgeon struck a match and took a long hard pull on his Marlboro, his narrow eyes visible from the orange glow of the cigarette.

"God, that took forever. I hate taking off those fucking old knees. The rest will be easy," he said, exhaling into the star-filled sky.

Energized by the break, we gathered back inside around the old lady. We were all ready to wrap this up and get out of there. The cameras began to roll, the surgeon cracked his knuckles and we all took a deep breath.

"OK," said the surgeon, "who's got the new knee?"

The response was silence. His question was met with blank stares.

"I don't have it," said someone.

"I thought you had it," said someone else.

"Well, I don't have it – check my desk!" and someone ran out while the rest of us just looked at one another.

She returned quickly.

"It's not on your desk."

"Well, check the shelf."

"It's not on the shelf."

"Do we have one anywhere?"

"I don't think so . . ."

"Check the whole building."

"I did. We don't have one."

"Well, start calling around," the surgeon pleaded.

The cameras continued to roll as phone calls were made to other regional hospitals.

"They've got one in Annapolis!" (40 miles away)

"Great – get it on a helicopter."

"The helicopter is already out."

"Then have someone drive it up." He pulled down his mask. "I guess that's another smoke break, everybody!"

I'm not a doctor but I knew this old lady was under anesthesia for a very long time and suddenly we were looking at another lengthy break.

"Oh, she'll be alright," the surgeon said, wishing the whole mistake wasn't caught on tape.

Another hour and a half would pass before the new knee arrived and finally, after many hours under sedation, the patient had a new knee implanted. Through the miracle of editing the whole operation looked routine and took minutes to complete.

***

In 1980, I led a delegation of fellow students to the college radio broadcaster's convention in New York City.

My good friend and the station's General Manager, Spiro Morekas, decided to drive us up to New York from Baltimore. The only problem was that his car was a death trap. I sat in the front. In the backseat sat Mike Pianowski and Mike Gerlach, two friends from the station. As rain descended on the New Jersey Turnpike, the two Mikes complained that their feet were getting wet. One pulled up a ratty carpet square and saw the road racing beneath them - the floorboards had rotted out! Spiro just waved his hand and plowed on. The decrepit car broke down for the first time in East Orange, New Jersey where we waited half a day for the repairs. Finally, back on the road, we headed for Manhattan and the posh fifty-two story hotel in midtown where the convention lay ahead.

Spiro Morekas, flanked by Ed Neenan, left (who created the cover design for this book) and Adrienne Kelly, right, on the streets of New York.

After a wild day of fun, I wound up in a Spiro's room with a bunch of guys watching *The Sensuous Nurse* on pay-per-view. The film ended at 3:30 AM and at the age of twenty it seemed like a good idea for the six of us to leave the room and scour the hotel for girls. We grabbed a small cooler of beers and set off.

We wound up playing Frisbee in the long, narrow hallway of the hotel until the noise of the Frisbee hitting the walls and our accompanying laughter woke up too many guests. Still wide awake, we went to the lobby at around 4:30 AM to drink beer and strategize.

Once in the lobby, we realized the rest of the hotel was quiet and everyone else was asleep so the chances of finding girls was minimal. Looking toward the elevators, I whispered, "Hey, I've got an idea. Let's go to the roof!" We drained our beers and piled into the elevator.

Looking at the buttons, I suggested we go to the 50th floor instead of the 52nd, that way we'd avoid suspicion in case anyone from the front desk had been watching us (which I'm quite sure they were.) I pushed the button for the 50th floor.

We laughed as the elevator whisked us up fifty flights rapidly, bending over to heighten the sensation of the alcohol. At the 50th floor, the elevator doors swung open and we poured out laughing. Immediately I noticed something strange. Blocking the hallway was a table and behind the table sat six well-dressed, wide-awake men. One of them, a tall blonde, spoke.

"Can I help you?"

I looked at my friends then said, "No, we're OK", and took one step toward the stairwell.

"I think you have the wrong floor," the man said.

I stopped, looked at him, then continued, "No, we're just going to the stairwell," I offered.

Then the man moved his arm, opening his jacket, revealing a large black gun in a holster on his waist.

He added, "Are you sure? Because *I* think you have the wrong floor."

Spotting the gun, we all froze.

I looked at the man and his serious friends and said, "You know, I think you're right. We *do* have the wrong floor."

With that we backed up and returned into the still-open elevator. When the doors closed, we all looked at one another.

"What the hell was that?" someone asked.

I responded, "I don't know but to hell with those guys. Let's go to the roof anyway," and pushed the button for the 52nd floor.

Two floors up there were no spooky men, so we got out and walked to the door for the stairwell where I thought we'd find access to the roof.

I pushed on the door, but it was stuck. I shoved it again. The handle turned but the door wouldn't open. Two of my friends assisted me and we gave it a mighty shove. Inside the stairwell slept a college student on a cot, passed out drunk. His body was blocking the door. We found him right where his friends had left him as a prank. Someone had written "I am a fool" on his forehead with a black magic marker. We laughed but he didn't wake up so we all filed past him and into the stairwell.

Down a short corridor I saw three steps up that led up to a door. On the door was a big red sign that warned, DO NOT OPEN. ALARM WILL SOUND.

I looked at my friends and said, "Well, we've come this far. If there *is* an alarm, we'll be gone by the time anyone gets up here."

I reached out, pushed the bar and the door swung open. We didn't hear an alarm. Instead, what we saw was a blanket of stars.

We were on the roof.

We stepped out and walked around, marveling at the beautiful view of Manhattan all lit up. Soon it would be dawn, and I suggested we go get our friends and have a rooftop photo session, which is what we did. It was a beautiful morning and we had a blast up there.

A snapshot from the infamous dawn rooftop photo session in New York. The clock in the distance reads 5:59AM. That's me on the left, holding up a Frank Zappa album I'd bought earlier the day before, with Ed Neenan, Cliff Gibbons, Brice Freeman and Larry Stenback.

Days later I learned what we'd stumbled onto on the 50th floor. It was 1980 and Senator Ted Kennedy was running for President. He was sleeping on the 50th floor and those were the Secret Service agents protecting him. You'd think they would have done a better job securing the roof. We were up there for about an hour with no one bothering us.

Ironically it wouldn't be the last time I ran into the Senator from Massachusetts. But that story was still a few years away.

On the ride back to Baltimore Spiro's car broke down again, this time leaving us stranded at a gas station near the Maryland-Delaware line. We all had had enough of his junker car and decided to abandon it right there. The only problem was we didn't have a ride home. The four of us were tired and needed to get to school the next day. Looking around, I spotted a priest and his friend filling up his car at the gas station. He had a very large car that would accommodate all four of us and our luggage. And now, he had a full tank of gas.

Mustering up my best manners I ambled up to him and said, "Excuse me, Father, but my friends and I are in a bit of a jam..."

The priest and his friend were headed to Washington but since Baltimore was on the way, the good man agreed to give us all a ride home. I sat in the backseat with the two Mikes and, since he got us into this mess, we made Spiro sit up front between the priest and his friend. The kindly priest took each of us back to our respective homes. I thank you again, kind stranger.

***

Around that time, I earned my first screen credit. A primetime ABC show called *That's Incredible* came to town and hired Flite Three for crew. The program featured true stories of bizarre behavior, amazing rescues and the occasional side show oddity after which the hosts and studio audience would shout, "That's Incredible!"

The producer asked Flite Three to provide him with a full remote crew as well as an associate producer. They looked around and since everyone else was either too busy or not interested, the company deemed me associate producer material. It was also in their best financial interest. That way, they'd charge a hefty fee, but not pay me anything more.

One day I'm holding an ashtray, the next I'm the associate producer on a network TV show. That's the television business.

Some of the glamour began to subside when I heard details of the story we'd be producing. A local guy had figured out a way to turn human waste into building bricks.

Immediately the jokes began to fly – shitting gold bricks, a brick shithouse, etc. I maintained a cool demeanor as, after all, I was now "management."

I took my new role seriously and dressed in a suit jacket and my best dress shoes the day of the shoot.

The main location was a playground where a small brown playhouse was built out of the fecal bricks. A group of children had been lined up to play in it to illustrate how safe the final product was. Unfortunately, a driving rain storm was rolling through the area and the little "log cabin" was under about a foot of water. But we were on a schedule and ABC was waiting for the segment so, on with the show.

"It'll be even better," said the producer. "If the bricks are wet and they still don't smell, it'll be great."

Well, these children would be the first to find out.

Our van pulled up to the playground during the height of the storm. As the driving rain and wind whipped at the windows, the side door of the van swung open and my boss looked at me. Every other day I was low man and I'd be expected to do the worst jobs like unload the gear in a driving rain storm but today I was the *Associate Producer*.

I looked at the water-soaked playground then down at my dress shoes then back at my boss and just smiled. My boss rolled his eyes then leapt out of the door with a mighty splash, his white sneakers disappearing beneath a large puddle of brown water. Then on cue about a dozen reluctant children ran out of a nearby house and splashed in and out of the tiny brown playhouse smiling and laughing and touching the bricks.

I was in the warm, dry van holding a clipboard when my drenched boss appeared in the doorway holding a set of keys.

"The producer says his car is illegally parked. He'd like you to move it for him, Mr. Associate Producer."

He pointed to a small red sports car parked in a bus stop about a hundred yards up a steep hill. I took the keys, popped open my umbrella and tip-toed off in the direction of the car while the crew shot more of the playhouse.

Confidently, I slipped into the producer's car and closed the door with a solid thump. Once again safe and dry and out of the storm I took a deep breath and smelled the fine leather. This was a one nice automobile.

I gripped the steering wheel, closed my eyes and dreamt of a great drive through Europe. I imagined myself turning down a sun-drenched corner in Monte Carlo as the rain pelted the windshield.

I slipped the key into the ignition. I thought about bringing the mighty engine to a roar when I looked down to discover that the producer's car was a stick shift. I had very limited experience with a stick that included ruining a jeep on the beach and that was about it.

My little fantasy was wiped away as my heart leapt into my throat. The rain was coming down in buckets on the expensive Italian car and I had to act. My boss was already pissed off at me. I'm supposed to be a member of the crew. They're paying good money for me to be here. I'd look like a loser if I couldn't do the one thing the producer asked me to do.

After all, how hard could it be?

As I sat pondering my options the windows started to steam up and it was getting increasingly hard to see. At the bottom of the hill the crew would be hurrying the shots in the pouring rain. Ok, Dugan.

Focus.

Push down the clutch with your left foot, give it a little gas with your right foot, turn the key then slowly release the clutch while giving the engine enough gas so it didn't conk out. Got it.

With authority I slammed down the clutch, turned the key and it started it up. As the throaty engine roared to life my heart began to beat through my chest. I reached down and dropped the producer's car into first gear.

I said a brief prayer then slowly eased up on the clutch and gave it some gas. The car charged like a lion away from the curb.

I began steering wildly as the car careened down the hill at a blazing speed. I must've given it too much gas.

I didn't want to take my foot off and hit the brake for fear of stalling it out. In the time it takes to scream "Yaaaaaaaa" I flew down the hill, narrowly avoided hitting a row of parked cars, went up on the curb, across a small lawn, up a small step and somehow managed to wedge the producer's car between the porch railing and the front door of someone's house.

And that's how I got my first screen credit – yeah!

***

As the program director of a college radio station I saw a few perks. One of which was the ability to meet celebrities as they came through Baltimore. I interviewed George Carlin, Nils Lofgren, the eclectic Robert Fripp, Rush's Geddy Lee and many others. I hung out backstage with The Ramones twice. They were only a few years older than me and the band was still struggling to make it big.

That's me, lower center, holding a microphone while interviewing Johnny Ramone
backstage at Martin's West in Baltimore. Above me sits Dee Dee Ramone, being
interviewed by JD Considine, a writer for Rolling Stone. Joey Ramone stands by
the door and Marky Ramone (partially obscured) sits to the left.

Photo by Richard Snyder.

The first time I saw the Ramones they played a small country bar
called the Seagull Inn. The bar was half full of the usual customers -
guys in plaid shirts and cowboy hats shooting pool - and half full of
punks with torn black tees and safety pins through their lips. This
was the very beginning of the punk movement and the local cowboy-
types didn't know what to make of them.

There was no trouble as the bouncer was my friend Adrienne's
boyfriend, a huge guy named Bryan, one of the biggest men I've ever
met. Thankfully Bryan and I were still friends even though I'd spilled
a full beer in his lap while playing air guitar at Kenny's Castaway Bar

during our New York trip. I was right next to the stage as The Ramones charged into one high energy song after another.

During the show a buxomly and very attractive brunette saw my backstage pass and squeezed between me and the stage, bent down and grinded her ass into my crotch. This type of behavior was rather new to me and I just enjoyed her enthusiasm, neglecting to put two-and-two together and that she was, of course, desperate to get into the dressing room. I just thought I was lucky. A stagehand saw her comely pleas for what they were and he beckoned her backstage and into the darkness beyond.

After the show I saw her and half a dozen other attractive women trying to entertain the band backstage. For punk rockers The Ramones were an odd lot. Joey, the lead singer, was still kind of shy and soft-spoken. We'd talk but his answers were brief and it seemed he'd rather be somewhere else. He rarely looked you in the eyes. He had the soul of an artist, though, and a deep desire to be heard. Despite his natural aversion to the spotlight Joey was a mighty oak in a leather jacket on stage and, as the front man for the band, he would eventually become known as the Father of Punk.

Dee Dee was the most prototypical punker, a total wild man. A speed freak who bounced around the room like a rubber ball, cackling, his maniacal laughter was contagious to everyone he met. It was Dee Dee who counted off the blindingly fast tempo of each song with his signature, "One Two Three Four!" But Dee Dee had the attention span of a flea and his mood shifted like a weathervane in a hurricane. A lot of what Dee Dee muttered was incoherent, but he seemed chuffed about it and people liked him. Even then he seemed like a gifted genius on a runaway train headed for an early grave.

Marky felt like a hired gun, a drummer trying to keep up with the madness, not quite comfortable in his leather and sneakers, images that would go on to become iconic and synonymous with rock and roll.

Johnny was the most talkative and became the de facto spokesman for the group, used to giving the press what they wanted. So naturally I spent most of my time with Johnny. We talked for a long time. He told me, "We feel limited because everything is so new. If we opened for Eddie Money, those people would think we were from Mars." None of us had an inkling the band would get credited with influencing so many great bands like Pearl Jam and U2, Green Day and Nirvana, the Clash and the Strokes. Or get inducted into the Rock and Roll Hall of Fame.

Me and Johnny Ramone, backstage.

Photo by Dee Dee Ramone

***

The Ramones Museum in Berlin. Photo courtesy of Luca Volpi.

Decades later, sitting at one of the two little tables outside of the Ramones museum in Berlin, curator Flo Haylor looks through the photographs I took of the Ramones at the Seagull Inn that night in 1979. One of them makes him sit up. It is a shot of Johnny playing a white guitar.

"You wouldn't believe the subculture that revolves around Johnny Ramone's guitars," he tells me. "This looks like the Hamer Johnny endorsed in an ad. But I've never seen a photograph of him actually playing it on stage."

We go into the museum and Flo gives me a personal tour. We stop at the Hamer ad. Sure enough, it looks like the same guitar in my photo.

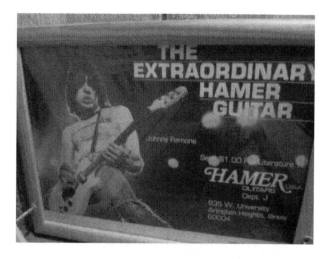

The Hamer ad in the Ramones Museum.

Joey Ramones in his classis lean-into-the-mic stance on left, Dee Dee Ramone center, in concert at The Seagull Inn

The photo I took of Johnny Ramone, the only known photo of him playing live in concert the Hamer guitar he endorsed in the ad, now proudly hangs in the Ramones Museum in Berlin.

"Could you please send me a copy of your photograph?" he asked. "I want to make it part of the permanent installation."

Flo tosses me a t-shirt from the gift shop for my son. These days a Ramones t-shirt is a piece of pop culture. But back when I hung out with them no one knew the Ramones would become legendary.

I walk out of the museum elated, thinking I finally recognized a good thing early on, even if I had no idea at the time.

Back then, one of the most fun times I had during my fascination with punk culture was with a band called The Plasmatics. The band is now largely forgotten but with songs like *Sex Junkie*, *Pig is a Pig* and

Butcher Baby, the Plasmatics were making headlines all over the world in 1981 for their outrageous behavior. My interview with Wendy O. Williams, the daring lead singer, was a blast. I still have my backstage pass.

My backstage pass to the Plasmatics show, proudly stuck to my college notebook.

Earlier that year, Wendy had been on trial in Milwaukee on an obscenity charge for simulating a sex act with a sledgehammer. Wendy's visual act was legendary. It consisted of smashing a working television on stage and chain-sawing a guitar in half while she sang. While these theatrics were going on Wendy bared her chest down to two tiny pieces of black electrical tape covering her nipples while the band ravaged through some pretty good punk.

I was twenty-one and had just witnessed the band's performance at Painter's Mill Music Fair, a three-thousand-seat venue where the round stage slowly spun around during the show. People in the audience tore each other apart for the guitar bits Wendy threw into the crowd after she chain-sawed them in half. I was glad I was watching from the relative safety of the sound engineer's pit next to the stage.

After the show I went backstage. Wendy bounced in, pulled a loose gray sweater over her huge bouncing tits, threw her arms around me and gave me a big wet kiss. We laughed and talked about the band, their recent appearance on *Good Morning America*, the band's troubles with the law and life on the road.

Then, out of the corner of my eye, I saw something strange.

I turned my gaze from the formerly-topless lead singer and caught a glimpse of a tall guy scowling at me. As Wendy continued to talk, I stared at this mad man. He had a really mean look, the kind of look a man has when he intends to rip your head off during some painful biker ritual.

Six-foot-seven, sporting a bright blue mohawk, a spiked leather bondage shirt, black high-top sneakers and a large shocking pink tutu, he saw me on the couch with Wendy and began charging across the room, eyes firmly locked on me.

He stomped up, stopped, and glared. I thought he might cold cock me right then and there without warning.

Instead, he smiled, stretched out his hand and said, "Hi, my name is Richie. Can I get you a beer?"

It was Richie Stotts, guitarist for the band, playing a little trick on me. With Wendy's theatrics demanding the crowd's attention on stage I neglected to even recognize Stotts. I shook his hand then enjoyed the cold beer he fetched and hung out the rest of the night with Wendy, Richie and the band.

I didn't know it at the time, but these encounters were laying the groundwork for me as a television producer and interviewer.

Around this time, I had started a blues show at the radio station and was asked to be the Master of Ceremonies at a concert at Painters Mill. The act was John Mayall and the Bluesbreakers, fronted by the legendary London bluesman himself.

On stage at Painter's Mill, sporting my vintage Goodwill tuxedo, getting ready to bring out the bands.

Photos courtesy of Rich Snyder.

The promoter asked me if I had any recommendations for an opening act. I immediately offered my friend Kevin Pope's band, The Snakedrivers. They were a top-notch local blues act. Pope was a childhood buddy and he'd become quite a drummer.

John Mayall had assembled a killer band for the tour including John McVie of Fleetwood Mac and Mick Taylor, formerly of the Rolling Stones, on guitar.

For some reason Mick Fleetwood was also on the bill the night I was MC.

My ticket stub for the Mayall show.

Months earlier Fleetwood and McVie had run into Mayall. Both longed for the intimacy of playing for smaller crowds and decided to tour with Mayall but Fleetwood dropped out at the last minute because he couldn't commit the time. Founding member of Fleetwood Mac, he was practically running the band at that time and was extremely busy. Fleetwood Mac had an album dropping in two days and he was planning a tour. Colin Allen had been the drummer for the Mayall gigs.

Yet Mick Fleetwood shows up for this one, obscure gig in Baltimore.

The big show was on June 16th, 1982. I took to the stage, said I was from WCVT, and the crowd went wild. What a feeling. I introduced the bands and it felt great to be there.

Toward the end of the show when, Mayall's band came backstage before an encore, I stood next to Mick Taylor and Mick Fleetwood. Here I am, Forrest Tucker's ashtray holder, and I was standing between two rock legends. I got a real earful as they complained to me about what an asshole John Mayall was being. Then Mayall returned to the stage. We could hear him begging the band to come back out and join him for an encore.

Mick Taylor, who needed the gig, reluctantly slunk back to the stage but Fleetwood just winked at me, bent down to the cooler, cracked open two cold beers and handed one to me.

"Fuck Mayall! I had one of the biggest albums of all time. I don't need this shit."

That was an understatement. By the time of this Mayall concert, Fleetwood Mac's 1977 release *Rumours* had sold an amazing 13 million copies worldwide and remains one of the Top Ten best-selling albums of all time. Fleetwood Mac was playing to sold-out stadiums.

Toasting his defiance with a clink of the bottles we heard Mayall on-stage begging the crowd, "Does anybody here know how to play the drums?"

This would have been an incredible, once-in-a-lifetime opportunity for my friend Kevin. Good lord, he'd get to play on stage with John Mayall, Mick Taylor and John McVie. But Kevin was partying backstage and never heard Mayall's plea.

I looked up at Mick Fleetwood, all six-foot-five inches of him, and laughed.

John Mayall played his encore without a drummer.

The next night, June 17th, John Mayall recorded the live album *1982 Reunion Tour* at the Wax Museum in Washington DC with drummer Colin Allen.

The next day Fleetwood Mac released the album *Mirage*.

Maybe Fleetwood was doing the Baltimore gig to knock off the rust the night before recording that live album with his old mates. God knows it would've sold a lot more with Mick Fleetwood's name on the jacket. I never did learn what pissed him off.

According to Mayall's website, Mick Fleetwood was "unavailable" for the 1982 reunion tour.

Less than two years later Mick Fleetwood filed for bankruptcy.

3

In the early eighties I could earn enough to pay for my college tuition while still going to school. Many parents of my generation wonder why their children can't do the same thing today. According to Forbes Magazine, college tuition has skyrocketed, costing an average of 500 percent more than it did when I when to school.

It's also harder than ever for students to find a good job. But back then I found lots of jobs to support myself and made enough to pay for college along the way. I worked at the airport selling foreign currency and travel insurance. I stocked the shelves of a greeting card shop. I was an editorial assistant at the Baltimore Sun newspaper.

And I was hired to be the on-stage host at a country music hall, the Master of Ceremonies at a place called the Country Music Showtime Theatre.

I was twenty I saw one man's dreams materialize and vanish over the span of a summer. I'd answered an ad in the newspaper seeking someone energetic with a good voice and, since I was the only one who applied, I got the job.

The owner had a dream to create his own version of The Grand Ole' Opry on the outskirts of Baltimore. He had grandiose plans of expanding it one day, turning it into his own national radio show.

That summer he booked some smoking hot musical acts like Charles Brown and David Grisman. The problem was he didn't know how to draw an audience.

He didn't advertise, he didn't give tickets away, he did virtually nothing to get people to come to his theatre. Each summer weekend I'd take to the stage, grab the mike and welcome the audience to the show - only the audience was always smaller than the band.

The theatre held over three hundred people but the biggest crowd he ever had was six - and the owner was one of them.

Undaunted, in mid-summer he married his girlfriend up on stage in a ceremony full of optimism. Predictably, the owner was soon very deep in debt.

As the summer wore on I heard lots of people, from the exterminator to the painters to the security guards, scream at him for money. I was the only consistent part of each show, appearing on stage at every performance, and he genuinely liked me. Somehow, he always found money to pay me, even after I saw others threaten him with bodily harm.

His lowest day came when he opened the soda machine and gave me the very last change he had. Maybe the guy didn't have a good business plan, but he had a big heart.

A few months after he opened the doors his theater shut down. He was broke, his vision was shattered, and my country music career was over. Just another man chasing his dreams, shot down in a blaze of glory.

Shortly afterwards I began to work for another man with a vision, only his fortunes turned out very differently.

A college dropout and used car dealer, Baltimorean David Saperstein

75

was stuck in his car during a snowstorm when he had a brainstorm. What if you could provide motorists with current traffic conditions on the radio and then franchise the concept across the country?

One of the reasons it took shape in Baltimore was the dedication of its first anchor, a guy named Chuck Whitaker. Chuck was a few years older than me, but he had grown up right around the corner from my childhood home in West Baltimore. He had escaped the old neighborhood and when I answered the newspaper ad for a producer, he recognized another young man trying to do the same.

Each weekday from 6:00 to 9:00 AM I'd produce traffic reports then attend college during the day only to return to produce traffic reports from 3:00 to 6:00PM.

Taking reports from us was a network of thirteen radio and two television stations. My role required me to sit behind an audio board watching the clock and send out traffic reports, timed down to the second, which were they then recorded and played back on the stations within minutes.

The way we gathered information about traffic conditions was far from the methods used today. This was an age before cell phones, road sensors or the internet. Helicopters were useful, but Saperstein felt they were too expensive and were often grounded in bad weather.

In the early days of Metro, we learned about traffic conditions by sending a handful of drivers out to look around.

When they saw a problem, they'd call me on a two-way radio and file a report, which I'd record on a cart machine. A cart was a clunky tape cartridge that looked like an 8-track tape with a hole in the bottom. One good feature of carts was that an engineer could record over and over on them, reusing the same piece of tape. Carts came in different lengths – thirty seconds, a minute, two minutes - and after they played, the tape would conveniently loop back around and cue itself back up at the beginning. Now this type of recording and cuing is all done on computers, but cart machines were used throughout the radio industry for decades due to their durability and reliability.

While I was watching the clock and recording reports from the field, Chuck would telephone various places around town like the Harbor Tunnel, the Transit and Traffic Department and the State Police, while constantly listening to two police scanners. That's how we gathered information for traffic reports.

Today, highways have speed sensors that feed reporters accurate information about how fast cars are travelling over a stretch of highway, determining how long a motorist will need to get from one point to another. There are countless traffic cameras online that show reporters what's happening. Cell phone users update apps to indicate accidents and traffic conditions. Traffic reports are a part of everyday life and are available through multiple platforms.

That vast system of traffic information has become so developed and accessible that the person giving listeners traffic conditions on the radio in your city might actually be sitting in Los Angeles or Atlanta. But in those early days we were literally inventing the genre, from whole cloth, first from Towson then from the Blaustein Building on Charles Street in downtown Baltimore.

A few of our feeds were live, where the on-air personality at the radio station would banter on-the-air with Chuck.

One station had a pretty funny DJ and Chuck would joke back and forth with him. This DJ liked to bait Chuck and sometimes got him off on tangents that would stray toward something off-color. After a few of these embarrassing incidents I took matters into my own hands. On the audio board is a button that activates a slate microphone, basically allowing the engineer to talk through the audio board.

During one exchange in which Chuck began to drift down an edgy path, I opened the mike and said, "Chuck,   as your producer, I'd advise you not to say that."

Chuck put his hand over his mike and said, "Dugan, as your boss, I'd advise you to shut the fuck up."

This exchange got a good laugh from the DJ who asked, "Who was that voice?"

Chuck replied, "Oh that's just Dugan."

The DJ didn't hear him and replied, "Who? Digger?"

Chuck paused, smiled at me and sneered, "Yes, that's right. Digger."

From that moment on I became Digger, Chuck Whittaker's sidekick on a local radio station.

Later that year Chuck was asked to be the Grand Marshall a big Fourth of July parade. When he came in to work the following Monday I asked him how it went. I thought he would've been thrilled with the honor of being the Grand Marshall, but he just hung his head and sighed, "All anybody asked me was, 'Where's Digger?'"

Chuck's back-up was a guy named Andy, a nice fellow with a good sense of humor. Andy's biggest flaw was that he was often late for work. In a job where we had to gather up-to-the-minute information and hit a series of marks for a network waiting for reports, that was bad.

One time Andy was late was memorable.

On Sunday December 14th, 1980, millions of people around the world paused in silence for ten minutes of silence to remember John Lennon who had been senselessly murdered less than a week earlier.

Thirty thousand gathered in Liverpool and nearly a quarter million converged on New York's Central Park, close to the scene of the shooting. For those ten minutes, every radio station in New York City went off the air.

I was deeply affected by the loss of John Lennon. When I first heard the news, I sat in the woods alone for three hours, stunned.

I was to meet Andy 45 minutes before the tribute in front of the building where Metro Traffic Control had their offices. I planned to do my ten minutes of silence in the office since I had to work that day.

So, there I was, standing outside the Blaustein Building, the tall chrome and glass office building in the heart of Baltimore, waiting. The building was locked for the weekend, but Andy had a key. Finally, he showed up minutes before the tribute only to announce that he'd forgotten the key. We had to be on the air soon.

So, at the appointed time, instead of hanging my head in silence along with the world for John Lennon, I was breaking into the Blaustein Building.

The building had 30 floors, a high-rise of chrome and glass. And when it was locked it was not easy to get into, especially with the number of bums and vagrants that shuffled around that area.

It was a Sunday, so traffic was light, no one was around and millions were observing a moment of silence. But Andy and I were noisy. First, we broke into the loading dock. Climbing a tall fence, we found a door. Knocking it down with our shoulders we finally forced it open and ran upstairs, missing the first scheduled report and John Lennon's ten minutes of silence.

Twenty years later David Saperstein sold Metro Traffic Control and its associated holdings for one and a quarter billion dollars. He's now considered one of the world's richest people.

I hope he fixed the door.

***

I finished my fourth year of college far short of the credits needed to graduate. Flite Three had offered me a full-time job a year earlier, when I was a junior, but I turned it down. Even though no one in my family had gotten a four-year degree I was determined to be the first. My big motivator was I wanted my parents to see me walk across a stage and get a diploma. I wasn't allowed to graduate with my high school class "for disciplinary reasons" because I caused a bit of a "disturbance" at a function. Go figure. So, I entered my fifth year of undergrad at Towson with 21 credits left to go.

As I wound down my college career I weaned myself away from WCVT to concentrate academically (some may say for the first time.) My last radio role was as a talk-show host. That semester I co-hosted a one-hour show weekly (or weakly.) It was called Media Makers.

My co-host Spiro Morekas was then, as now, a very good radio sportscaster. Spiro and I chatted on this live call-in show every Tuesday night and we took turns booking the guests. The problem was Spiro and I had very different tastes and booked very different people. For example, I booked a professor named Dr. DeBrabender to talk for an hour about the meaning of life. Spiro didn't say much that night. Then Spiro booked a guy named Keith Van Eron, the goalie for the Baltimore Blast indoor soccer team. I confess I didn't have a lot to ask Keith. In fact, I only asked him one question:

"Keith, you're a soccer player, a goalie... It's your job to have people kick things at you all day, every day. Do you ever get a defensive attitude?"

With dead eyes the six-foot-one pro goalie looked blankly at me and simply replied, "No" then turned back to Spiro.

I don't recall much else about Media Makers and I doubt anyone in

Baltimore does. I do know that people still fondly remember WCVT. Even though I worked every single day of the week - juggling school, the radio station, a full-time job, my internship at Flite Three and an active social life - those crazy days were some of the best times of my life.

***

I barely squeaked by that final 21 credit semester. All I needed was a passing grade in COBOL, a computer class whose final project consisted of a shoebox full of punch cards. I ended the semester with barely an idea of the concept of computer programming, but I knew that if those cards stayed in order and went cleanly through some giant ass computer everything should be cool. All was well until I dropped the box on the way to the lab.

I hurriedly stacked them all back together and handed them in, knowing I was fucked. I begged the teacher to be kind as I shook his hand. He knew it was the only thing left between me and my diploma.

He put my stack of punch cards into a feeding tray and they sped off into the giant blue computer. I heard shredding and clanging. Big red lights flashed. Then the whole thing clunked to a stop. The professor began removing a giant side panel as I backed away smiling, offering a lame "thumbs up." I'm not sure how long it took him to get the thing back to working order but in the end, he took pity on my and gave me a D. That is a passing grade, my friend. And with that I was out of college.

With an uncertain future before me, I took my newly acquired free time to contemplate my next move.

By then I had a college degree in mass communications with experience in radio, television and newspapers. I pondered my future and it made sense to me to select one of these three disciplines to pursue. If I didn't make a conscious choice I'd simply take the next job that came along and leave it to fate, not choice. One day I'd find myself down a path I had not chosen and wind up stuck, like so many people do. I'd be old plastic bag shredding in the wind on a fence.

This was my time. My chance. I better think this through. Alone.

On the campus of Johns Hopkins University there is a small sculpture garden set back amongst the trees. The garden is a quiet oasis, a tranquil spot with marble statues of animals connected by a winding stone path. It was designed as a contemplative place. I found it was everything I was looking for as a destination for my new mission to plan my life and career.

Near the center of the garden lies an owl, a symbol of wisdom and, according to the small metal plate at its base, this Benjamin Burano sculpture was created in 1960, the same year I was born. I took this coincidence as an omen of good fortune. I sat on that owl and began to think. I just thought. All day.

The next day I returned and thought again, all day. I sat on that marble owl off and on for four straight days. By the fourth day I had made some observations about myself and came up with a plan for my future. If you ever find yourself at a personal crossroads I highly recommend this simple approach. Just sit and listen. For as long as it takes. I learned a lot about myself sitting on that owl.

Radio was my first love as it had been the reason I chose to attend Towson State University. I loved being behind the mike, listening to music and being a DJ. But as I considered that as a career I thought about the friends I had who'd gone that route. It was a life of constant change, moving from city to city, always chasing a bigger market. Job security was slim. Jobs were lost with regularity as radio stations changed their formats to chase bigger demographics. My friends were often fired without warning, through no fault of their own. And nobody made big coin unless you were Howard Stern. No, I wanted something better.

I strongly considered newspapers. I had worked at the Baltimore Sun for a while as vacation relief for news desk guys on leave. It was a cool place. I had earned a reputation as a dependable person and was offered the coveted job as editorial assistant on the sports desk, a springboard to sports reporter. I loved the camaraderie of the newsroom and the way breaking news rippled through the building. I loved election nights as reporters scurried to predict the outcomes. I enjoyed writing words as an art form and the way it could move people. But the internet was the beginning of the end for most metropolitan newspapers. The whole medium was on the decline. And it didn't help that papers were no longer being run by journalists but by big businesses chasing a profit. There did not seem to be a bright future for me there either.

Television was different. Cable TV was exploding at the time and that growth meant more jobs and more opportunities. During my time at Flite Three the mystery surrounding how television production works had faded away. I was confident I could hold my own. Sitting on that owl I declared to myself that it would be a career in television for me.

Then I closed my eyes and began to envision a tangible goal. I decided that I wanted to complete a dream I had years earlier sitting on my parent's couch. I wanted to create a documentary of my own that aired coast to coast. I pictured a huge billboard in the sky, one that everyone in the country could see – and I wanted to fill it up. I wasn't sure what my documentary would be about, but I set upon myself to figure out how to make documentaries and get them on the air.

I now had my goal and I could see it from afar.

I would not be that plastic bag blowing in the wind.

Sitting on the owl I closed my eyes, envisioning a distant mountaintop. I would become a television producer. Every career decision I made from that point on would be with the same goal in mind. It was my mountaintop.

I felt that if I held onto the vision of a mountain in the distance I could take small steps toward it. I knew there were unknown valleys, dark woods and many obstacles between me and my mountaintop but if I could look up occasionally and see it I could keep moving in the right direction. Thanks owl.

***

Armed with a long-term goal I set out to tackle a few short-term goals. At the top of the list was a new source of income. I put out calls to all my friends for help. Meanwhile I started my own austerity program, cutting back expenses to the bare necessities.

I was poor, broke and hungry. My only telephone was the pay phone two blocks away in front of a liquor store. But it was a happy time.

There was one crazy, steamy August Saturday night. It was wretchedly hot – one of those stick-to-the-sheets, no-breeze Baltimore summer nights - and I was keeping my window air conditioner off to save electricity. Nearby, the Baltimore Museum of Art was screening foreign films in air-conditioned bliss. I ambled over there, laid down my last six dollars and planned to sit through two back-to-back screenings. The first film was set on the French Riviera, with beautiful women in flowing gowns exiting long limousines, the perfect escape to fill my idle imagination on an empty wallet. But to my dismay they emptied the theatre between shows. Bored and broke I was outside in the heat again only to see that the once-empty museum courtyard was now filled with beautiful women in flowing gowns exiting long limousines.

I asked one of the passing women, "What's going on?"

"A charity ball," she replied, smiling, the streetlight glistening off her low-cut sequined gown.

Suddenly I had an idea. I raced home and found the brochures I picked up at the BMA the previous Wednesday, the one day of the week they'd offered free admission. On the back of one brochure was a list of donors. I memorized the names of all the women. Then I donned my Goodwill tuxedo, pinned on an obscure war medal I'd picked up at a flea market and marched back into the hot night air to the museum.

At the door I was asked for my ticket. I launched into a charade of hand gestures and gibberish, sprinkling in equal measures of high school French, lyrics from an old Maurice Chevalier record and the names of the women from the brochure, all accompanied by panicked looks and grand gestures toward the entrance. I was banking on the fact that few people in Baltimore spoke French. I knew for a fact no one would go get a rich woman upstairs from her husband to say there was this French guy at the front door dropping her name. In a few minutes time I managed to convince the gatekeeper that I was in fact a French ambassador who had misplaced his ticket. Fearing an international incident, they let me in. That night I spent a few hours in cool luxury, savoring a free steak dinner and an open bar, dancing with a few of those gowned women who howled with laughter at my charade.

Shades of my father, the wedding crasher.

***

I needed to break out and land a freelance gig. The next step up on the pecking order from grip was the audio guy so I tried to find work as one. In those days, much as it is now, it comes down to who you know.

Kim Mendenhall, my post-college girlfriend, got me my first freelance job. (She was not the Kim I later married and got drunk with Gore Vidal a decade later.) Like me, Kim Mendenhall was aspiring to a career in TV and we had just graduated college together. But she was a lot sharper than me this point. And I do mean sharp. If she was a pencil, I was a stone. Kim had been landing a lot of freelance work and was fast on her way to becoming an accomplished camera operator.

She occasionally worked for a local producer named Mr. G. He was an ambitious, seat-of-your-pants style producer who would bid on jobs and then try to figure out how to accomplish them. He had gotten a contract to shoot a sports show interview and I rode Kim's coattails onto the crew. The shoot was for a local baseball program centered on the Baltimore Orioles. It seemed that, after years of negotiations, the show had finally landed an interview with the reclusive owner of the Orioles, a lawyer named Edward Bennett Williams. It was a big coup because Williams never ever gave interviews. If he did it was on a respectable national news program like 60 Minutes to discuss some high-profile case he'd won in court. Williams was one of the first "super lawyers." He was a pillar of the Washington DC power establishment and seemed always to be friends with whatever President was in power. But he preferred to be one of those behind-the-scenes type of guys. He didn't need press. Certainly not local Baltimore press.

But this point in his life was both rare and special. Williams and the Orioles had just won the World Series. In fact, Williams had the honor of part-owning the NFL Super Bowl XVII winning Washington Redskins (along with co-owner Jack Kent Cooke) and baseball's World Series winning Baltimore Orioles in the same year,

1983. No sports team owner has done this before or since.

In short, this was Mr. G's biggest shoot. Ever.

Kim was there when Mr. G was assembling his crew list. He had assigned her, two other experienced and trusty camera operators and a lighting director but he still needed an audio guy. Kim recommended me. She vouched for me. That's how it works. You get into that inner circle of freelancers by word of mouth from someone trusted. Of course, I had never run audio on a TV remote production in my life, but I had been a late-night DJ at an obscure college radio station and hung around a bunch of TV shoots. I got the gig.

Kim and I showed up at the location and were led into an exclusive downtown club – dark-paneled walls, over-stuffed chairs, subdued lighting and a spectacular view of the city skyline. Kim went right to work setting up her camera, running cables, helping with the lights. I walked over to the audio gear and just stared at it. It looked like a strange puzzle, a tangle of black spaghetti and mysterious little boxes. I begged Kim to help me out. She told me she would when she got a chance, but we only had a very short window of time to get this interview on tape and get out.

I fumbled with the headphones, tweaked some knobs and tried to look busy. Then in walked the owner of the Orioles with the host of the show. The tension in the room doubled. I watched the lighting guy wresting with a glare from the windows as Kim and the rest of the crew readied their cameras. This shoot demanded a crack audio guy, somebody fast and slick who really knew their craft. Instead it had me – a totally incompetent novice fumbling through his first gig.

Mr. G scooted between two tables, leered at me and barked, "Mike 'em up!"

OK, I thought, somewhere in this pile of black spaghetti is a microphone. But nothing looked like a microphone. Kim reached into the pile of gear and pulled out two wireless lavaliere microphones and handed them to me. All eyes were on me as I approached the owner and the host. Thankfully the host knew what to do and he put on both his mike and the owner's. I scrambled back to my station and slipped on my headphones.

Mr. G nervously turned to me and asked, "Are we good?"

I looked at Kim.

She mouthed, "Can you hear them?"

I nodded yes.

Mr. G snapped, "Roll tape!" and we were off.

The one key instruction I wish I had received from someone was that if the audio sounds odd, it is *solely* the audio guy's responsibility to stop the taping and tell someone. Well, the audio wasn't good. The wireless mikes were picking up some very bad interference. I looked at Kim. Her back was to me. She was focused on her job with the camera. So, I looked at Mr. G. A soft light bathed his face in glory as he watched what was, for him, the interview of a lifetime. I twisted and tweaked the little knobs to no avail. I just shut up and convinced myself that since everyone else was happy, this must be the way things go.

The following Saturday Kim and I waited for the big show to air on our local TV station. We turned to the channel and there it was.

"Turn it up," I asked enthusiastically.

"It is up," she said.

Then I saw the message at the bottom of the screen, 'Audio Problem Not in Your Set.' As we struggled to listen to the muffled interview of Edward Bennett Williams I cringed into the corner of Kim's sofa. We could hear it, but the sound quality was bad. Kim just laughed and turned it off. Later that afternoon I called Mr. G and apologized. He told me not to worry, these things happen. I'll always appreciate his generosity.

On location with Mr. G in a bowling alley during those early days. We were shooting a show called *The Duckpin Challenge* and by this time I had graduated to camera operator. After studying another guy light a few episodes, I went to Mr. G and asked if I could light them. I would charge a little less than the other guy. He liked to save a few coins and, as such, I wound up 'double dipping,' getting paid as both the lighting director and as a camera operator. Hence the grin.

The cheesy host of this dreadful bowling show once cracked up the entire crew by greeting the viewing audience then asking his co-host, a former pro bowler, to join him up on the alley. As the co-host approached the host intoned, "Look. He just doesn't feel comfortable coming up here without his balls in his hand." Every camera operator, including me, laughed so hard our cameras shook violently and for about 30 seconds. The director couldn't take any of our shots.

***

I must laugh as I look back on some of those stories from the early days. God, I screwed up a lot. It's a wonder I ever made it in TV. Instead I should've been drawn and quartered.

Leaving the Berlin apartment, I feel like I could use good stiff a drink. I find a bar just a few footsteps from my building's door. Tiny pendant lamps create pools of light over each table. A sharp dressed young businessman sits next to a bearded artist clad in black. A Japanese couple laughs while two tables away a young German woman picks at her meal in silence as she reads a book. The bartenders speak Russian to one another while a young German man at the other end of the bar laughs at a private joke. Other diners congregate in the back, each group steeped in their own animated conversations. I seem to be the only American in the bar.

Oranges, lemons, limes and a ginger root behind the bar combine their scents with a bright ginger-citrus smell. The paintings on the walls are full of color with sad faces, an homage to German angst. Although the bar is vibrant and alive with the sound of people it also feels peaceful. There is a positive energy here and I like it. I settle in and order a scotch on the rocks and, picking up my silver pen to write, I notice my hands are sore from typing. Instead of more writing I decide to drink up and go for a walk.

When I go to leave I fumble in my limited German by asking for the check, but I forget to ask the bartender to round up the bill for a tip. I was told that, unlike back home, it is considered improper to leave money on the bar. The whole bill exchange happened so quickly that I find myself exiting without leaving a gratuity. I feel terrible. I want to go back but I can't explain myself. Later I think about the bartender and about coming to a foreign land and I reinforce one thought that is certain about jumping into the unfamiliar.

At some point you're bound to make mistakes.

***

Kim Mendenhall and I were both enamored of a new art form that had recently emerged: the music video. Kim and I decided to form our own company to create them. We called it The DMO – The Dugan-Mendenhall Organization. We bought a box of business cards. I'm confident you've never heard of The DMO because we never produced anything. Except one lawsuit.

I don't recall how we first met the band. I'll call them *Brown Doughnut* (not their real name) but their de-facto leader – a guy I'll call Baker – worked at the same place as my brother. Brown Doughnut was recording at an upscale local studio named Sheffield, and they wanted a music video to go with their new big single.

Kim and I met with Baker and the rest of the band, listened to the demo of their song and began to come up with ideas. They liked us. On the spot we decided to work together. We had no contract, just a handshake.

Kim and I began to work night after night on how we could visually bring their song to life. I talked to Baker a lot on the phone. We decided on a budget for the project. Kim and I would not get a fee, but we'd get credits on the production, something we could use to build our business. So, all the money went up on the screen. The band liked a lot of our ideas, offered some of their own and after a few weeks, we had what we felt was a solid script.

Then, without warning, the band dumped the DMO. Sheffield had offered them a package deal for the music recording and the video and they took it – along with our script.

With little recourse I marched off to the local small claims court and filed a claim. For ten bucks you could get your day in court but for an extra twenty bucks a State Trooper would personally hand-deliver a subpoena to Baker at work. I felt this shock value was worth every penny and signed up for the cop. I would have loved to have seen the look on his face – and his coworkers' faces – when a uniformed Maryland State Police Officer showed up and slapped him with a subpoena.

Soon enough our day in court arrived.

It was sunny but freaking cold – likely late fall or winter. I wore a suit with a big grey flannel overcoat I'd picked up at the Salvation Army. Accompanying Kim and I was her roommate Luffy, who came to testify that we had in fact put many hours into the script. Not quite knowing what to expect, the three of us entered the courtroom. Across the room sat the band and their lawyer, a chisel chinned guy named Ed in his fancy suit and big dark blue flannel overcoat.

I don't know if you've ever been to small claims court, but it is living theatre. The case before ours involved an old man who accused another old man of stealing.

Old Man: "He stole my toilet."

Judge: "How do you know he has *your* toilet, Mr. Jones?"

"Oh, it's mine all right! He don't have no terlet and now he's got one - and mine's gone!"

Mercifully the bailiff announced, "Dugan Mendenhall vs. Brown Doughnut." Kim and Luffy took seats on a bench at the front of the room. The band took seats on the corresponding bench on their side. Ed and I stood at tables in front of the judge. Then I heard members of the band laughing. They though Luffy was our lawyer and when they realized I would be representing us I overheard one of them say,

"Ed will slay him."

I looked up at the judge and on his cue, we stated our case. We had done the work and couldn't get what we were promised – credits as the creators. So, we calculated our value to the video community and multiplied it times the hours we put in and came up with a dollar number. Not high, but a few thousand dollars, which was a lot of money to us.

Ed immediately went on the attack. He balked, pointing out the lack of a contract. The judge turned back to me. Knowing I wasn't a lawyer the judge explained that I now had the opportunity to call any witnesses if I wished. In his statement Ed said the band did not dispute the fact that we did indeed work on the project so there'd be no need for Luffy's testimony. I looked around the room for someone to call to the stand.

"Baker," I replied.

Baker took the witness stand and was sworn in on a Bible "to tell the truth, the whole truth, and nothing but the truth, so help you God."

I stepped in between the tables like the lawyers I'd seen so often on TV, clasped my hands behind my back, took a deep breath and asked,

"Baker, is it not true we discussed this project at length on   the telephone?"

"No," was his simple reply.

He was lying of course. Not wanting to give him any kind of a platform, I simply shook my head, returned to my table, waved him away.

"No further questions, your honor."

Now, either the judge was impressed with me for some unknown reason or simply happy I wasn't wasting his time, but he clearly looked at me with something of an appreciation. Then the judge asked Baker to please step down and return to his seat. He then called counsel to approach the bench. Ed walked up to him and believing I should too I quickly followed. The judge spoke to us in a voice loud enough for everyone to hear,

"I'd like to see the two of you in my chambers."

Yikes! What had I done? The judge stood up and the whole courtroom rose to their feet. I looked back at Kim and Luffy as the judge, Ed and I left through a side door together. As I exited Kim squirreled up her lower lip at me. It was all I could do to return the puzzled gesture as I left the courtroom and headed into the hall.

In his chambers the judge loosened his robe, put his feet on the desk and lit up a cigarette. Ed and I sat in chairs in front of his big oak desk. He took a long pull on his cigarette, exhaled and spoke.

"I don't want to decide this, Ed. How about a settlement?"

Ed's eyes narrowed as he replied, "They won't give them a cent."

The judge turned away, as if wrestling with a thought, although in retrospect he probably just wanted to enjoy a cigarette and that's why he called for a recess in the first place. The three of us sat silently as the smoke curled under his green glass desk lamp. The silence became deafening.

The entire time I was in his office I didn't say a single word.

Soon we returned to the court room. Everyone stood for the judge and then sat back down with a mixture of tense curiosity and anticipation. The judge briefly recapped my story, talked about the tough decision and finally said,

"The court finds for Dugan Mendenhall, 100 per cent, plus court costs."

Bam. As he slammed down his gavel, a wave of joy came up in Kim,

Luffy and I and a curtain of despair descended on the band as we all rose and left while the bailiff called the next case.

As I turned and grabbed my big grey coat a thought dawned on me: what would happen if they didn't pay us? I needed to find out before I left the courthouse. I gave the keys of my trusty Dodge Dart to Kim and asked her to bring the car around. Meanwhile I ducked out the back and went down a hall to the court clerk's window to ask my question. The clerk told me that because I now had an order from the court, if the band doesn't pay, I could do something called "attach a lien," basically snatch Baker's paycheck if I knew where he worked. And of course, I did because he worked where my brother worked.

Happy as I've ever been, I left the courthouse and stood outside on the sidewalk with my eyes closed, my face in the warm winter sun, waiting for the car. The sun felt so good and as I took a deep breath I was thrilled with my improvised courtroom victory.

But suddenly I had the feeling I was no longer alone. I opened my eyes, squinted, and saw the band's lawyer Ed right in front of me in his big blue coat. He squared off, clearly embarrassed that he'd lost to an amateur. "Of course, you know they won't pay," he spat.

I looked across the street and saw the band, cussing and shaking their fists at me as they slunk toward their car. I turned back to Ed and poked his chest through his big blue coat. "Oh, they'll pay, or I'll slap a lien on his wages so fast it'll make your head spin!" then pointed across the street toward Baker.

Just then the Dodge Dart pulled up, I hopped in and Kim peeled off leaving Ed and the band in a cloud of Baltimore dust. They did pay up, but Kim and I never managed to work on a music video. A year later Kim Mendenhall and I went our separate ways. She made a big name for herself in television in San Diego. But I have good memories - and at least one of those DMO business cards still floating around.

Part Two

A Life in Television

As a freelance camera operator in Baltimore in the mid-80's, I worked regularly for WJZ, Channel 13. Jerry Turner was a beloved anchorman and Channel 13 was top dog in local news in those days. Fortunately for them, they never let me work the news as breaking a false story like a nuclear leak on Channel 13 would have sent the city into a tailspin. But I did get a lot of work shooting and producing their public service announcements. I also got a lot of work from a show called *Evening Magazine*.

WJZ was owned and operated by Westinghouse at the time, which also owned stations in about a dozen other cities. Each station had their own version of *Evening Magazine* and they shared stories. Each market had two local on-camera hosts, one female and one male. In Baltimore it was always Donna Hamilton, a real pro, and some other dude. There was a succession of changing male hosts, most of them with small talent and big egos. They should've called the show *Donna and the Prima Donnas*.

One day I might be going out with a producer to shoot a story, another day I might be shooting what we called "ins and outs" – where the hosts go somewhere and record the little bits that tie the stories together.

Here's the way ins and outs worked at *Evening Magazine*. First, the two co-hosts would appear together, on location, then, after the first story, one would appear, pretending to have just watched the segment the viewers saw and then talk up the next segment. This would go on, back and forth, throughout the half hour, then they'd both appear together at the end to wrap up the show.

Typically, the show would open with one of them saying something like, "Welcome to *Evening Magazine*. Tonight, we're at The Hovel, a great downtown place for lunch."

The other might say, "Speaking of food, our first story tonight is about a new twist on key lime pie. Mmmm, that sounds good, doesn't it?" followed by grins, nods and overt belly rubbing.

Then we'd change the shot and they'd pretend they just watched this segment on pie, rub their bellies some more and set up the next story.

The day we worked at the coffee shop I was the audio guy. By now I knew what I was doing. I had a pair of wireless microphones and put one on each of the hosts. Each mike ran to a little transmitter, a small black box each host had clipped to their belt or back pocket, so it wouldn't show on camera. I had two little receivers that plugged into a clunky ¾-inch tape deck, which was in turn connected to a camera by what we referred to as the umbilical cord. I would don my head phones, sling the deck over my shoulder with a strap and try to stay close enough to the cameraman so we didn't pull each other over as we moved around. Each of the field tapes held twenty minutes worth of material.

At one point, after many takes of opens and teases, I called for a tape change and everyone else took a short break. I rewound our tape, checked the quality, then popped it out, wrote on the label the date, the crew, the location and the show number. Then I put a new tape into the deck. Since these tapes were always being reused and recorded over, I had to "stack" the new blank tape, basically fast-forwarding it to the end, then rewinding it back again so the tension during our recording would be consistent.

The protocol was to lay down a minute of bars and tone at the head of each tape, so the editor could properly set up the color and audio levels. Color bars were generated by flipping a switch on the side of the camera, but I didn't have a tone generator, so I just recorded bars and whatever was coming in off the wireless microphones. I sat there for the minute it took to record bars and this is what I heard in my headphones:

In my right ear I could hear Donna and the female producer over at a side table talking about what a jackass this male co-host was. They called him a womanizer and worse. And I concur - he was a dick.

In my left ear I could hear the dick. He was in the next room hitting on a young saleswoman; smooth talking her in a sleazy, seductive lounge voice. Judgment confirmed. Total dick.

To make it worse I knew the scumbag was married with children as we'd been to his house. And now both conversations, the one at the table and the dick's sleazy pick-up, were recorded on tape.

Realizing what I'd done – and being a freelancer who wanted to work again – I rewound the tape, turned down the mikes and re-recorded over it, destroying the evidence of the co-host's philandering ways and the brewing conspiracy against him.

On another shoot I had a run-in myself with that very same asshole dick. By this time, I had moved my way up to camera operator. I was sent on a rare shoot where the talent (aka dick) was also the segment producer. So instead of a producer in charge, the dick was calling the shots.

The dick had an idea to do a segment on child molestation and perverts. I can't imagine why. Maybe he found some statistics somewhere and pitched the idea. Anyway, at his insistence, we went to a residential street in an affluent Baltimore suburb and rolled out of the van.

"Here," he said. "Get a shot of me walking up the sidewalk with this house in the background."

"What are you going to say?" I asked.

"I'm going to say that any house in a quiet neighborhood could be the house of a child molester."

"You can't do that. You're implying that *this* house has a child molester in it!"

"It's cool – just do it."

"No," I argued. "There's no way I'm going to shoot that."

Just then the homeowner came out of his garage, taking a can of trash toward the curb.

"Hi guys – what're you shooting today?" the unsuspecting homeowner asked.

The dick responded: "Oh, we're just shooting a segment on the high value of homes in this beautiful neighborhood," he lied.

The homeowner smiled contentedly and waved as he walked back into his garage. The dick then turned back to me and sneered.

"Now do it!"

I replied, "Only if you get the blessing from the show's executive producer. Then I'll shoot it. Otherwise, no fucking way."

Fortunately, while the dick was lying to the homeowner, I had an extra moment to think. I was now adamant that I was not going to take the hit for his stupidity. If he wanted to do this foolish stand-up in front of some innocent man's home, then he needed some approval from a higher authority. And I knew the sniveling coward wouldn't phone in the request. I just stood there on the sidewalk toe-to-toe with the him while he fumed. His eyes glared at me. He was the talent! How dare I question his judgment? He was used to getting his way by intimidating people, but I squared off and stood up to him. The dick wouldn't make the phone call and finally relented. We shot his stand-up in front of some generic woods.

Like most of the male co-hosts on Baltimore's *Evening Magazine* he was gone from the show in a few months. But I managed to keep both my integrity and my job as a freelancer. In fact, I've only seen him on TV once in the last thirty years. I guess others saw what I saw in him.

Morale of the story: Don't go down with a dick.

***

We all bend the rules occasionally. You may have heard the saying: IT'S EASIER TO ASK FOR FORGIVENESS THAN PERMISSION. This is no truer anywhere than the television business. Another saying is JUST GET THE SHOT. Come back with the goods. No shot, no TV show.

Sometimes the desire to get the goods takes you to the edge. A good example was on another *Evening Magazine* shoot.

We traveled to Easton, Maryland for a story. Maryland's Eastern Shore is another world from Baltimore, a land of farmers and hunters. A rustic place where camouflage is couture.

And the locals are suspicious of people from "across the bridge."

The story we were covering was about an Easton woman in her 30's known as The Mayonnaise Queen. She had inherited millions from her great grandfather's condiments empire. She and her boyfriend had tried to parlay the inheritance by moving 440 pounds of cocaine from Florida on a private plane, something like John DeLorean-comes-to-Maryland. She was caught and we were trying to tell her tale.

Now, this was not like working for the news side of the house. This was an old story by news standards. To complicate things, the producer on this shoot was competent but very urban and very superstitious. Everything spooked her about this shoot - the long drive over the Bay Bridge, the rural Eastern Shore, the spookiness of the drug story. At one point, clutching the little hang-down strap in the van, she admitted that she was in over her head. Once again, I was the audio guy. Fortunately, our camera operator was a cool guy named Anatole - a level-headed, experienced shooter - and he helped assure her we'd get what we came after. We'd come back with the goods.

As we pulled into Easton, it became clear that the reclusive Eastern Shore residents wanted absolutely nothing to do with this TV crew from Baltimore. The one interview the producer had lined up got cold feet and cancelled on her.

We were on our own as we tried to find the $750,000 house where the Queen and her boyfriend had their operation before it was seized by the feds. Reportedly they kept loaded guns in every room.

Far off the highway, down a nondescript road, we came to a driveway cordoned off with yellow police tape and "No Trespassing" signs. We stopped the engine. It was dead quiet outside. Too quiet. Spooky quiet. To make the scene even creepier, a low fog clung to the ground.

It was late morning but in the haze, we could just barely make out the shape of a house at the top of the driveway. Anatole surveyed the scene from the van and said, "Let's walk up to the house."

Freaked out, the producer wanted no part of it. The yellow tape read: "Crime Scene – Do Not Enter." She was right to be cautious. But Anatole remained calm.

"We came this far," he said. "Let's just walk up and get some shots."

I slipped on my headphones and connected my boom pole (a long stick with a directional mike on the end) to the camera. Using it with headphones I could only hear what the mike was pointed at. It creates a strange sensation, especially in a tense situation like this. I was in sensory deprivation and couldn't tell what direction sound was coming from.

Anatole reached for the van door. As the side door creaked open and a large bird flew out of a nearby tree, startling all three of us. Anatole stepped out of the van with the camera. I could hear his feet crunch on the oyster shell driveway. Since the umbilical cord between his camera and my tape deck was only about six feet long, I had no choice but to follow him. OK, I thought. Here goes. I'm illegally entering a crime scene. There's a first for everything.

Next, I heard footsteps scrambling toward us quickly. I was not sure where they were coming from. Turns out it was the producer. Scared to be left alone in the van, she suddenly ran up from behind and grabbed my shirt. She was now cowering behind my back, peeking over my shoulder. The three of us slowly inched our way toward the house in the fog.

The producer pulled my headphones aside and whispered to me to stop. Anatole and I looked at her in the creepy silence. She said she had to tell us one more thing before we went any farther. It seems that earlier she had spoken on the phone with the owner of the plane that was used in the crime. Apparently, a local guy had bought the plane at auction, and the producer had arranged for us to visit the small Easton Airport to get some footage of it. But the new owner also developed cold feet. As she relayed her phone conversation to us, I could hear fear in her voice. He'd told her, "If you come anywhere near this plane, I'll shoot you!"

If things weren't freaky enough, now we had an actual death threat. Once again, Anatole took charge. "We are going up this driveway and getting what we came after," he whispered.

We crept up the driveway in silence. We slowly ducked under more yellow police tape. I held my boom pole out in front of me like a lance. All I could hear was the sound of our own footsteps crunching on the shattered pieces of oyster shells. It was chilling as we slowly, methodically, made our way up the driveway through the fog to the house, Anatole in the lead, me connected to him via the cord, the producer anxiously clinging to my back. I turned up the volume in my headphones until the oyster shells sounded like mini explosions as we walked.

We had to cross over yet one more line of police tape to enter the back yard. When Anatole crossed that line, the producer must've felt like she'd tempted fate enough. She ripped herself away from my back and bolted back down the driveway to the relative safety of the van. Anatole pulled up the tape and I slipped under it behind him. The two of us were now alone, well beyond police lines. We began to survey what we saw. In the yard, towels were slung across lounge chairs around the pool as if the occupants had left in a hurry. Cocktail glasses still set on the end tables. Leaves swirled on the pool's surface. In the distance there was a private pier barely visible in the haze. You could hear a pin drop.

Anatole crept up to the house and peered into a window. The table looked set for lunch. Just then a seagull swooped down on us and squawked, scaring the fuck out of us. Anatole brought his camera up to his eye.

"Just get some shots and then let's get the hell out of here," I whispered.

"Okay, I'll be quick," he replied.

It felt like an eternity while Anatole stood there taping. Finally, we hustled back down to the van where the producer sat, visibly upset. I was just happy to get away from the house without being hassled by cops.

Even with a death threat looming over us from the plane's new owner we went to the airport anyway. Fuck him. With no interviews and just a few shots of an empty house we didn't have much of a story.

The people at the airport were stand-offish and firm. No one would tell us where the plane was. And the death threat felt even more real.

Finally, we'd seen enough and we headed back on the road for the two-hour drive back to Baltimore. We never did get an interview or a shot of the actual plane. But we did get exclusive shots of The Mayonnaise Queen fancy house and the way it was frozen in time. The story was cobbled together with footage of the trial, the empty house and a file shot of a similar plane.

Now it's fun to watch a story on TV and look for what visuals they have and try to figure out what they wanted and couldn't get.

One other experience with yellow police tape became memorable - for all the wrong reasons.

We had an interview connected with some story downtown at the federal courthouse. There is a lot of security around those places. I imagine judges and witnesses are often threatened and intimidated in big court cases. Oblivious to this, we simply went about our business of getting in, getting the interview and getting out.

A professional TV crew on location doesn't travel light, at least in those days we didn't. We had all the required lights, extension cords, audio gear, spare batteries and tape, as well as the camera, tripod and anything else we thought we might need. On the way out, I was dragging a large black anvil case full of portable lights when I said to my colleague I'd go get the van.

I left the big black metal case at the top of the steps in front of the courthouse. Instead of waiting there he went back inside to get the rest of the gear. Since parking at these places is limited as all nearby spots were reserved for judges, cops, officials and everybody *but* a TV crew, I had to park a few blocks away. By the time I got back to the front door, a whole team of security personnel had surrounded the light kit and were cordoning off the area with yellow caution tape while another bevy of cops started shooing people away from the building. They thought my light kit was a bomb.

That time I was lucky I got back in time to explain and salvage the kit or else I would've had to pay for a replacement out of my own pocket after they'd destroyed it. I once knew a producer who was flying through Rome with a suitcase full of rented walkie-talkies on his way to a film location. He left the heavy bag unattended for a minute to go to the bathroom and when he returned the cops had taken it away, x-rayed it, seen it was full of electronics, taken it out to a nearby field - and blown it up.

There was at least one *Evening Magazine* shoot where I was the camera operator and, despite all my efforts, I did *not* get the shot.

The story was about Frostbite Sailing. We went out on one of those long, America's Cup-style sailboats from the Annapolis Harbor. The call time at the dock was 4:00 AM.

'Call time' means the time you are standing in place, ready to work. You have already "shit, showered and shaved." You've said your prayers, had your breakfast, gotten dressed, kissed your loved ones, left your house, parked your car, drunk your coffee and completed whatever else you must complete in the morning. You've gotten the batteries off the charger, done any paperwork, gotten directions and contacted your crew. You've checked out your gear, assembled the package, packed it up and are ready to roll. So, at the designated call time you are standing in place, with your gear, ready to work - preferably fifteen minutes early. If you want a long career in television, then understand this rule: *You can be early – but you can't be late.*

In short, don't fuck up the call time.

I had gotten to the station at about 2:20 AM to load up the gear. It was the dead of winter and I knew we'd be out on the Chesapeake Bay all day, so I took extra camera batteries. The batteries at that time were large black bricks and rechargeable. Each one weighed about six pounds. Taking extra ones would mean hauling around extra weight but I needed the insurance. I knew once we sailed I was out for the day and couldn't return for more. I took every available battery off the chargers and slipped them into a large canvas bag. These bags are nicknamed 'run bags' because once you're out shooting you need to be able to toss all the loose gear into the bag and run to the next location.

We arrived at the pier at 3:45 AM. We knew our captain immediately as his boat had the only activity in the frozen harbor. We could hear his crew chipping the ice from off the boat.

Man, it was cold. It's cold anyway in Annapolis during the winter but in the dead of winter, just before sunrise, with a steady breeze off the bay, it's cold as fuck.

Fortunately, by this time, cameras held the recording machine all in one unit and I wouldn't be tethered to anyone. I'd use the microphone attached to the camera for ambient sound. Although all this added weight to the camera at least I could move freely.

I started shooting immediately as the sailing crew began to free the seventy-five-foot vessel from its frozen moorings. I shot their meeting and then boarded the boat for a dawn launch.

Soon we set out of the harbor and into the open waters of the Chesapeake Bay where we encountered another multi-million-dollar boat, like ours, sailing with a full crew. Even though it was as cold as it was, the two boats were to race, hence the term "Frostbite Sailing." I was there to document this expensive and grueling hobby.

The two huge vessels swung in the strong breeze as they angled side by side approaching the agreed-upon starting point. But there was a problem. Under the conditions the boats were swinging too closely to one another. I shot the captain of the other boat as he screamed, "Fall off! Fall off!!"

Just then the water between the boats disappeared and they brushed one another at full speed. The impact threw the heavy camera from my shoulder as I stumbled on the slippery deck. I caught it and righted myself, but in the confusion, I wasn't sure if the impact caused my thumb to hit the record button on the side of the lens thereby stopping the camera at what was a most dramatic moment. I looked for the little red record light. I was still rolling. Good. At least I had one cool shot.

After that close call, I positioned myself in a hole near the stern so that only my waist was above the deck but at least I could have some support. Now understand I am a city boy, not a sailor. I wasn't used to the way sailboats moved.

I zoomed in as the crew quickly turned the silver crank handles to move the mainsail. While I was zoomed in, my right eye was in the eyepiece looking at a close-up while my left eye was closed due to the now-blinding sun coming over the horizon. That was unfortunate because when the boom swung what I had been standing on moved beneath me about 90 degrees. It's like your eyes are closed and suddenly the floor is now the wall. That tossed me like a ragdoll. To make matters worse I was top-heavy due to the camera. The result was slamming my ribs into the hard wood on the other side of the hole. The momentum carried the heavy camera off my shoulder and toward the cold, deep waters of the Chesapeake Bay. I just barely managed to hold onto it with my fingertips. I winced from the pain of my now-bruised ribs. I believe that was the moment I learned to shoot with both eyes open.

Shooting on a tarmac with a camera roughly the same size and weight of the one nearly ripped from my hands while shooting frostbite sailing on the Chesapeake Bay. Note the black brick battery on the back end.

I'd been out for hours getting beat up when mercifully the race hit a halfway point. Everyone stopped for a while. No rest for me though as I was lowered over the side into a small rubber Zodiac to get shots of the ships from afar. This was where I began to have real problems.

In the Zodiac I swapped out camera batteries only to learn that each one of the thirteen extra batteries I had held no charge. It wasn't unusual to find one or two bad batteries in a bunch because they are often abused on shoots, quickly recharged repeatedly and they lose their memory over time. But to have all thirteen crap out on me in the middle of the bay was a real shock. It turns out that I'd arrived at the station so early that day and there was a late-night shoot the night before. The batteries were not on the charger long enough. The extreme cold was also a factor since it can affect all the gear. But the staff back at the station wouldn't be interested in excuses. As a freelancer you need to return with the goods if you want to work again. There was nothing I could do. I was literally dead in the water.

In the end, the editors cobbled together a brilliant cut that simulated the end of the race with earlier footage. The viewers never knew the difference. It wasn't the first time, nor would it be the last time, I was cursed in post-production by an editor.

Here's an excellent example of my incompetence that resulted in an editor wanting to kill me. Around this time, I was sent on another freelance shoot, this time for Maryland Public Television. I was told to document a song by a musician named Buckwheat Zydeco and his New Orleans-style band. I showed up at a local bar called the Eight by Ten for their afternoon sound check. They were to play one of their songs a few times and I'd shoot it from different angles. It was just me with one single camera.

This type of shooting is called 'film style.' As opposed to having multiple cameras shooting at the same time with a variety of close-ups and wide shots, like you would in a TV studio or at a football game, this technique has a single camera documenting the action in a wide shot. The action is then recreated over and over again for all the other angles needed, and then the footage is edited together as if it were a single event shot from a variety of angles.

I set up my wide shot, also known as 'the master shot,' and looked through the viewfinder. Since the shot was so wide, I could see all of the multi-colored stage lights and thought it'd be cool to add a star filter to the camera. A star filter basically makes bright lights appear to burst out in a star-like pattern. I tried it out and it looked great. The band was ready to go, but since they were up on a stage, I was looking up at them and didn't like the angle. I set the focus on my camera, then raised the tripod legs up as high as they would extend, about eight feet, so high that I could no longer see through the viewfinder. I stood on the camera case, but still couldn't get high enough to see through the viewfinder. And the band was getting restless. But I knew the shot was cool as it was a wide shot.

Confident I'd set my focus I hit the record button and told them to begin. They launched into the song and that's when I made a critical error. I thought it would look even cooler if I slowly rotated the star filter as they played, giving the lights some movement. As I did this I was also inadvertently changing the focus, but I couldn't tell because the camera was up so high.

The band ran through the song two more times, and I shot close-ups. Confident that I'd done a solid job, I gave the band the thumbs up, packed up my gear, delivered the tapes to the station and went home. The next day I got a call from the producer. Since the wide shot was so grossly out of focus, it couldn't be used. He had to edit the entire song just using the close-up footage. What should have taken him about forty-five minutes to edit took him ten hours because he had no master shot to cut back to.

He delicately pointed out my error. "Fuck you, Dugan! You completely and totally suck. I hope I never see your sorry face again, you dumb fuck. I've got an idea. Why don't you just get out of the television business altogether because, if I have anything to do with it, you'll never ever work in this town again!"

I knew I would never work for that producer again. That's the way it works in the freelance world: burn me and you're out. There are too many others waiting to take your spot.

I did manage to somewhat redeem myself on a subsequent MPT shoot, albeit for another producer.

I was back to running audio. We were assigned to go out on a fishing boat from Ocean City during the White Marlin Open, the world's largest billfish tournament. We left at dawn for an all-day excursion out in the Atlantic. This time I wasn't the one worrying about camera batteries.

A wrinkle in our plan came up the moment the boat left the dock. The camera operator, a nice guy named Mike, hit the deck inside the cabin like an old throw rug. He was severely seasick. His face was the color of pistachio ice cream.

It took about an hour to get out to the fishing area and once we arrived, the crew got moving but my partner was totally out of it. He couldn't peel his face from the deck. Luckily, I knew both roles. I picked up the camera and did both my job and his. I managed to hang in there all morning and was good until lunchtime when one crew member took out a tuna fish sandwich. I got one whiff of that and I too was heaving over the side. But I did manage to collect myself and got everything we needed.

I'll never forget how Mike sprang back to life the moment that boat tapped the dock at the end of the day. That's just the way it works. You must look out for one another.

Camera operator Mike Fevang and producer Margaret Sullivan back on the pier after Mike's "miraculous recovery."

The best thing about doing this kind of work is that you never really know what the day will hold. One day I was told we were shooting an interview for *Evening Magazine* with the singer Suzanne Vega. I had heard about the concert and knew the leader of The Byrds, Roger McGuinn, was her opening act. I told the young producer, but she had never heard of The Byrds.

I was the camera operator on the shoot - and there is a definite hierarchy on a crew - so I knew I was stretching the limit when I asked if I could interview McGuinn. The show's executive producer told me to go ahead. After all, if the interview was any good, they'd get a free segment. I was paying attention to how a producer works, learning how to conduct a television interview and honing my own skill set. But I was underprepared for McGuinn and asked some banal questions. Sorry Roger. But I did learn a lot from the experience. And it was fun to sit down and chat with one of the heroes of my youth. Roger McGuinn was very gracious. One cool thing he told me was Tom Petty had it right, naming his band after himself. McGuinn confided that if he'd done the same thing with The Byrds, he'd be playing stadiums instead of opening for others on the bar circuit. I have no doubt he was right.

Roger McGuinn on the left, me on the right, after I did a horrendous interview.

Working as a freelance camera operator was rarely boring. On one *Evening Magazine* shoot we were sent to cover a local appearance by an African dance troop. The venue was a long, squalid hall, not air conditioned and hot as hell in the Baltimore summer heat. The dancers ratcheted up the temperature, dancing in wild unison for the cameras, sweat flying off in every direction. We interviewed the organizers and choreographers. Satisfied we had what we'd come for, the audio guy and I took our gear to the van while the producer continued to get a few details from the organizer. I was sitting in the van with the big van door open, trying to catch a breeze when a young African man from the dance troop left the building and began to get into the van with us. He whispered to me, "I come with you. I come with you." He had a desperate look on his face.

He managed to get one foot up in the van when three other guys from the dance troop reached in and pulled him back out to the sidewalk. They laughed and said he was just kidding. But before they pulled him back into the building, I looked into his eyes. I knew he wasn't kidding. It all had happened so fast I wasn't sure what was going on but looking back I'm convinced the young man was trying to defect into the *Evening Magazine* van. I never knew what became of him.

***

Berlin is full of contrasts. It has a dark past but a modern vibrant heart. I'm tired after days of writing so I search for a movie theater to catch a film. There is an English-language film festival a mere two blocks away from my apartment.

Wandering over to Kino Babylon I take in an Arabic film about an obscure dictator. Leaving the theatre, a light snow begins to fall, dancing silently in the streetlights. I look up and smile. The scene reminds me of another February night decades ago, outside a more notorious theatre in Washington. It was the night Ted Kennedy thought I was sent to kill him.

Six years after the infamous rooftop photo session in New York, I was sent on a shoot in DC to cover none other than Senator Edward Kennedy of Massachusetts. That night I was a one-man band, the term used when a camera operator is sent out with no audio guy. This sucks. And it sucked even more because cheap ass Maryland Public Television hadn't upgraded to new equipment. I was hauling a heavy load. 20-pound camera, 20-pound ¾-inch tape deck, umbilical cord, 25-pound battery belt and a sun-gun light and microphone attached to the top of the camera.

Ted Kennedy was attending a charity auction and I was the freelancer covering the event for MPT. The auction took place at Ford's Theatre in the heart of Washington, right under the balcony where President Abraham Lincoln was killed by an assassin. Now Ted Kennedy was standing under that balcony. Ted, who himself helped to bury two famous brothers, President John F. Kennedy and former Attorney General and presidential hopeful Bobby Kennedy, also both also killed by assassins.

I stood on the stage and took a half step back. My heel caught the edge of the stage. Top-heavy from carrying 70 pounds of equipment, I began to fall backwards and off the ten-foot stage and into the darkness below. Thankfully Margaret Sullivan, my producer, saw what was happening and grabbed me by the shirt at the last possible second before I fell.

That was the moment I silently pledged never to go out as a one-man band again. And I never have. But that wasn't the defining event of the night.

Relieved after the near-disaster, I sat down the gear and placed the camera on a tripod. I noticed my camera battery was fading fast. Since I'd been carrying a heavy load I had no spare battery on me.

Margaret was busy setting up an interview with Tip O'Neill, then Speaker of the House but also the MC for tonight's charity auction. As a freelancer I was responsible for the camera equipment and I didn't want to leave it unattended. But I had no choice.

I sprinted out to the production van at full speed. Fortunately, I'd arrived at Ford's Theatre early that night and had gotten a great parking space right in front of the theater. I ran to the street side of the van, threw open the driver's door, tossed in the dead brick battery, grabbed a fresh one, then slammed the door, all in one fluid motion. As I was racing toward the back of the van, Senator Kennedy was leaving Ford's Theatre. Kennedy stepped off the curb and into the small space between the back of the van and a parked car. I flew around the back corner of the van and slammed straight into his chest at full speed. It was dark and the collision surprised us both. But Kennedy recoiled in horror, gasping for breath, his famous face in full shock, mouth wide open, eyes revealing true panic. I knew I'd hit him hard, but I didn't understand the look on his face. For a moment we both just froze and stared at each other.

In Washington DC, Ted Kennedy was akin to royalty. Nicknamed "The Lion of the Senate," Kennedy was protected, even revered. I knew that by the time we stood there frozen in that moment of shock, Ted Kennedy had endured a lifetime of stress few of us could fathom. He'd made so many speeches, so many appearances - there must've been so many faces in the crowd – all with the history of his slain brothers in the back of his mind. He'd run for President and experienced Secret Service protection but there was none present this night. It must've been drilled into him to never let his guard down. He likely had nightmares about the horror that might appear out of the shadows one night. In that frozen moment, he looked down and in my hand, was a mysterious black object. Was it a bomb? He couldn't know it was just a harmless camera battery.

All I managed to muster after standing there awhile was a feeble,

"Excuse me, Senator."

I raced past him and back to my abandoned camera.

For 25 years I recalled this story at parties to my friends, but it was always a mystery to me why Kennedy reacted so strongly that night. Now I think I understand.

After a very public life and five decades in the United States Senate, Edward Kennedy died in 2009 at the age of 77. After his death the FBI released over two thousand pages of previously secret documents revealing a constant series of death threats aimed at him, spanning a period from 1961 to 1985. The threats came with regularity and some were chilling.

> "We are after you," read one letter. "One of us will get you."

Thousands of threats like that would wear down any man's soul. Walking down the streets of Berlin on a cold winter night I finally understood the look of terror on Ted Kennedy's face. I knew the public figure, but I did not know the man. In life it is not uncommon to encounter someone you think you know and be puzzled by their reactions, but we rarely learn what really may have been going through their mind at the time. Now, with the knowledge of those FBI documents, I may have finally come to understand what went through Ted Kennedy's mind on that dark winter night so long ago.

The way he looked at me in that moment was one of sheer terror.

He thought he saw the face of his assassin. Me. His assassin. That's still unbelievable.

I get on the U-Bahn to Potsdamer Platz. The train is crowded but I manage to find a seat when many people leave the train at Alexanderplatz. I sit across from a variety of strangers including an attractive young woman reading a book. At the next stop I get up to give my seat to an elderly woman who has boarded. At Potsdamer Platz I exit along with hordes of people. I pause briefly on the long narrow platform to look at the signs wondering which end to exit from when suddenly a young man moves and stops right in front of me. Speaking rapidly to me in German he has a low tone. I don't understand what he's saying. A flood of possibilities flip through my mind.

"Could you spare some change for a brother?"

"Are you lost? What are you looking for?"

"Why did you give up your seat to that woman?"

I look at him. Then I notice the attractive woman who was reading a book is standing with him. The young man speaks again. Again, I don't know what he's saying.

"So, do you want to buy some marijuana or not?"

"How long will you be in Berlin, Mr. Bond?"

"What's the frequency, Kenneth?"

I have my iPod earbuds on and I feign disinterest, moving past the couple quickly, away from the stairs and back down the long narrow platform. My pace is hurried. As I walk I realize I have no idea where I'm going or if they are following me. I'm not even sure there is another exit at the far end of the platform. I pick up my pace, weaving through a throng of people when I see a small glass elevator with three elderly people inside. There is room for one more person. The glass door looks like it is about to close. I take two big steps toward the elevator, slip inside and the glass door closes behind me. In an instant I am whisked one flight up to the plaza and disappear into the crowd at Potsdamer Platz. I never see those two young people again. I still have no idea what he said to me.

I think about what it's like to be a foreigner in a place where I don't know anyone or speak the language. I suddenly realize I'm all alone. If I'm injured or attacked I'll have to figure it all out on my own.

Fuck 'em. I don't think that young man back there meant me any harm, but I'm not totally convinced. My emotions swell up inside. I think again about Ted Kennedy and his terrified look when he bumped into me.

I must calm down. I came to Potsdamer Platz to visit a much larger film festival, the Berlinale, one of the world's great cultural events. It's all very glamorous and I enjoy the energy but I'm not looking to be lost in another film tonight. Instead I walk around looking at the faces of strangers. Centered in sparkling Potsdamer Platz, I am in a dynamic open space ringed with gleaming skyscrapers and incredible modern architecture. It's hard to believe that for four decades this area was a no-man's land occupied by a wall that divided the city. But I'm still a little spooked and I don't linger long.

Back underground there are no turnstiles to get on the train. Like the trams above people just get on and off at leisure. I have a pass in my pocket like I expect most people here do but no one seems to check the entire time I'm in Berlin. The trains and trams are in the business of moving people around safely and efficiently on the honor system. I really like that.

The U-Bahn whisks me back beneath Berlin. The train turns and tosses me back and forth as it changes direction. Much of the scenery is a blur. I know those feelings of fear stirred up by the young stranger will paralyze me if I let them linger. I take a deep breath and push all those feelings away. Life holds challenges and fear can be a very big obstacle. I remind myself that I am safe. I came to Berlin to get something done. Finish this damn book. I'm determined to finish it.

4

On September 26, 1986, I was a freelancer on a shoot for the National Security Agency. President Ronald Reagan dedicated Ops 2 A&B, two gleaming blue-glass buildings that would become an icon for the agency. The NSA TV Center staff needed an extra camera operator to cover the ceremony. The parking lot in front of the two new massive buildings was cordoned off to accommodate a large crowd of employees and guests. I had to arrive hours early since the Secret Service would eventually put us on lockdown.

Lockdown occurs at media events the President will attend. Basically, you get your camera in position, stand there and stay there until the President leaves. This can be many, many hours. It's exhausting but it's part of working in the Washington area. Another camera operator recently told me that a buddy of his worked President Obama's second inauguration ceremony and was in lockdown on top of the Newseum for twelve hours without food or a bathroom break just so he could get one brief shot of the President's motorcade coming down Pennsylvania Avenue. You can't reason with the Secret Service.

At the NSA ceremony I was placed up front, about twelve feet in front of the podium. Two cables linked my camera back to a rented production truck. One cable sent images from my camera back to the truck and second cable allowed me to communicate with the director and crew via a headset. Typically, these communications are bundled together in one big cable called a triax, along with other things like 'return' so I could push a button on my camera and see the program live and 'tally' a little red light that appears in my viewfinder letting me know my shot is currently being selected as well as electricity to power my camera. Since we weren't running triax I had to power my camera yet again with one of those large black brick batteries, the same kind that scared the hell out of Ted Kennedy seven months earlier. At least there was very little chance of me running full speed into Reagan. The Secret Service would make damned sure of that.

I got myself into position, slipped on my headset and pointed my camera at the podium. I heard the director in the truck say my camera looked good. All I had to do was wait for lockdown. Realizing that I might be there for a while I asked the director if it would be a good idea for me to get another battery as a back-up and he agreed. I tossed down my headset and sprinted for the truck. I didn't get three steps before a Secret Service agent grabbed me by the arm. All he said was, "Walk. Don't run."

That's me in the lower right center of the photo. I'm wearing a white Home Team Sports cap, bending over my camera, while President Ronald Reagan gives his dedication speech at NSA.

The Secret Service are under an incredible amount of pressure every day and as a result are a skittish bunch. Fortunately, I was able to walk to the truck, get another battery and walk back to my spot before lockdown.

Fortunately, we didn't have to wait too long. President Reagan's helicopter, Marine One, landed in a nearby parking lot and he was whisked to the podium. Immediately I learned of a problem.

The director in the truck told me over the headset that the truck could no longer see my shot. Something must've happened to my camera cable. There was no way we could run another cable through the crowd, besides we were on lockdown. Despairingly, the director began to call the show using the other available cameras but clearly, he was missing 'the money shot,' since my camera was in the best position for the podium. Luckily the camera I was given had the capability to record onto tape and, thinking about all possible contingencies, I had brought a tape with me. I slipped the tape into the camera and began to record. I was able to get good close-up shots of Reagan and, since I was the only camera up-front, I could spin around and get applause and reaction shots from the crowd. Reagan delivered a brief speech and was once again whisked away. After his helicopter left we were free to move around the parking lot.

I broke down my camera position and delivered my tape to the truck where an exasperated director and a harried producer were conducting a heated discussion about some post-ceremony editing.

A few days later I received a call from the guy who booked me. He said my tape saved the show since I had great shots of the podium and they could cover up the edits using my shots of the crowd as cutaways. For once I didn't fuck up!

As a result, NSA offered me a fulltime job. These were the heady days when Reagan's Secretary of Defense Caspar Weinberger was known as "Cap the Ladle" for advocating large increases in defense spending, throwing money at every idea that came up. With NSA flush with new financial investment they were in a hiring surge. I was faced with a difficult decision as I was already booked to take a half-year position in Saudi Arabia where I was expecting to net a year's salary in six-months, tax free. Thinking about the long term I took the NSA job instead.

A shoot on the White House lawn with, from the left, Larry Bowers, Ray Kreiner, Tom Pokorny and me. By this time, I was the producer. Yeah.

Located halfway between Baltimore and Washington, NSA was one of the few DC-based places that made it easy to get to every day from my home in Baltimore. Washington DC is notorious for bad automobile traffic, often listed as the worst in the nation by people who track that kind of stuff. I don't think it's been out of the Top Ten cities in the US for bad traffic since the car was invented. So thankfully I didn't have to deal with that every day.

NSA hired me not as a camera operator but as a producer. It was the next rung on the ladder and that was my incentive to take the job.

On my first day I was given what seemed to be a simple assignment. I was asked to record a brief address for newly hired employees. The address was to be given by LTG William Odom, a three-star Army general and the Director of NSA. The Top Dog. The Big Cheese.

I was told another producer had written the script and it was already approved all the way up the chain. Because I was the new guy someone thought it would be a good idea for me to take over the project. All I had to do was to go to the Director's office with a camera operator and politely watch as the General delivered his address to the camera. The plan was for the General to read from a teleprompter, a device attached to the front of the camera where words appear using a two-way piece of glass, creating the illusion of eye contact with the viewer while reading a script. Newscasters use it all the time.

I was told to have the General start behind his desk then get up and sit on the front corner of his desk as he reads to give the piece a little movement. It sounded simple. Just like dozens of corporate shoots I'd done before. My camera operator Steve had been at NSA for decades and assured me that this shoot would be 'a piece of cake.' Of course, it was anything but.

Early the next day we arrived at the General's office. We were let in by one of his staff members. The General was next door in his big conference room receiving his customary morning briefing about what was going on in the world.

Steve and I set up the lights and put the camera together, complete with the teleprompter preloaded with the script. We checked out the equipment and decided we were ready.

Steve slipped out to go to the bathroom while I relaxed on a big leather couch in the General's office. Suddenly a side door burst open and the General stormed into the room. He headed straight for his desk to get some papers than stormed back out but not before glancing over at the stranger on the sofa. No one told me I should stand up when a three-star General enters the room. I didn't know shit from Shinola. It was my first week on the job. I just smiled and tossed him a casual wave from my perch on the couch.

When Steve returned I told him the General had popped in and he'd looked mad about something. Maybe the meeting wasn't going well. Just then that side door flew open again and in came the General and another Colonel. Fortunately, by then Steve and I were already standing. Since the General was preoccupied by something, Steve and I just waited for him to speak first. After a brief consult with the Col, he swung around and scowled, "What's all this then?"

I was now the producer, so I took charge. I smiled and said, "We're here to record your address to new hires," and I handed him a printed copy of the approved script.

He sat behind his desk and began to read. After a few seconds he took the script and threw it against the wall sending a shower of paper across the room.

"I'm not reading this Goddamned script!" he shouted, following with, "and I bet you want me to sit on the edge of the desk. Well, it makes my ass hurt and I'm not doing that either!"

After this outburst I saw Steve hiding behind the camera. As the producer I again stepped forward.

"Yes sir, I do want you to sit on the edge of the desk. You see, the desk is a psychological barrier between you and the viewers. We want you to seem friendly and accessible."

He grimaced then said, 'All right I'll do it. But I'm saying what the hell I want to say, not that hogwash in the script."

I didn't have any stake in the script.

"Fine, sir. Just start out behind your desk. When you feel comfortable, move around and sit on the corner to finish your address to the new hires."

We rolled tape and he began a rambling awkward speech, but he did get up in the middle of it and sit on the edge of the desk. When he finished he turned around to the Colonel and asked, "How was that?"

Hey, wait a minute I thought. I'm the fucking producer here. I ambled up to the desk, sat down beside him and grabbed him by the arm – that part of a General's arm with a bunch of stripes on the sleeve – and in a calm but firm voice I said, "You're going to do it again and I'm going to tell you why."

As he slowly turned toward me, the medals on his chest glistened in the lights. He looked at my hand on his uniformed arm then up at me. I could see black veins pulsate in his temple. He gave me a look I can only describe as a man who could have me killed then dump my body in a place where no one would ever find me. The truth was that he could probably do it, too.

LTG William E. Odom, Director of the National Security Agency 1985 - 1988. Note the stripes on the arm of his uniform where I grabbed him.

So, in a moment of wisdom, I let go of his arm. But I didn't blink. I smiled, and offered a few words of direction. The General did the speech again. It was better, but not great. I asked Steve if he got it on tape. "Oh, we got it," he replied.

I could tell Steve's his tone I'd be pressing everyone's luck if I asked for a third take. I thanked the General and he quickly left the room with the Colonel to discuss some more pressing world matters than my dumbass address to new hires.

Steve and I started packing up the gear. When we were just about finished, with Steve in the hallway and me once again alone in the General's office, Odom returned. By this time, he had cooled down considerably. He moved behind his desk and stood at the window looking out, hands clasped behind his back. After a few moments he spoke to me without turning from the window.

"I know I'm not very good on camera," he said. "I want to be better."

"I can work with you," I offered.

With that he sighed, nodded, sat down at his desk and began to work.

I never did get the chance to coach him as I was just starting a job buried ten levels of management below. A year, later General Odom retired from the Army and NSA. He lived another twenty years and became a frequent contributor on CNN as a military analyst. But he never got much better at speaking on TV.

Other assignments I had at NSA weren't nearly as hair raising. For example, once I found myself on a long shooting trip to Honolulu with Steve. Steve was a road veteran and knew how to get things done. This trip would have at least one weekend built into it. As the producer I saw to that. If you're going someplace cool, build the trip around a weekend, otherwise you'd never get to take advantage of the opportunities available.

Steve had been to Honolulu on the island of Oahu at least a dozen times, he'd never been to any of the other Hawaiian Islands. I declared we needed to go to another island for our weekend. Steve agreed.

On Thursday of that week we stopped by a travel agent who put together a nice package for us on the island of Kauai, including beachfront accommodations and a Mustang convertible. Our short flight would depart early Saturday morning. Excited, we both looked forward to a fun weekend adventure.

Saturday morning arrived and we happily showed up at the Honolulu Airport about an hour before our 8:00 AM flight. It was one of those crisp, beautiful, sunny Hawaiian mornings. At the ticket counter we met Mr. Chin, a man who immediately changed our mood.

"We're here to check in for the 8:00 AM flight to Kauai," I said with a smile.

"Oh, it's gone. See? There it go . . ." he replied, pointing to a jet taking off on the runway.

"What?! It's only 7:00 AM!"

"When they get full, we send them," he said, half ignoring me as he looked at his computer screen.

"Well, what are we going to do?" I asked.

"Hmmm . . ." Mr. Chin grimaced as he tapped his keyboard. "Ten o'clock full . . . Eleven o'clock full . . . I might be able to get you on 2:00 PM flight – maybe – but I no promise!"

I looked over at Steve. He was a few feet away, oblivious to the situation. I felt our fun weekend slowly evaporating into the crowded confines of the Honolulu Airport. I looked down at my tickets. The travel agent didn't tell us about this policy of sending the planes early. I looked back at Steve standing at the far end of the ticket counter. He was wearing a Hawaiian shirt, plaid shorts, sandals, a camera around his neck, all topped off with a New York Yankees baseball cap. The big lug – he needed this break. I had an idea.

My eyes narrowed as I turned my attention back to Mr. Chin. With a straight face, I leaned over the counter and said,

"Excuse me Mr. Chin, but if the Ambassador over there doesn't get to Kauai for his meeting, there's going to be trouble."

I nodded toward Steve. Chin looked up from his computer and looked at Steve. For extra emphasis I leaned all the way across the counter and put my lips next to Mr. Chin's ear and whispered,

"You know? Trouble."

Chin then turned his attention to me. I moved back, stood tall and looked him in the eye without blinking and gently nodded.

Chin didn't waste a beat. Nobody likes trouble. He wasn't about to call my bluff. He gathered the rest of the counter staff in a quick huddle, then came back to me, smiled and said,

"We'll get you on the next flight!" handing me two boarding passes.

I walked over to Steve who asked me what was going on. I replied,

"We're on the ten o'clock flight. I'll tell you what happened when we get to Kauai."

The Ambassador and I explore a cave on Kauai.

On Kauai we checked into our Poipu Beach hotel and decided to drive up the east side of the island. We had a balls-out convertible and the weather was perfect. Kauai was lush and green, unspoiled and underdeveloped in those days. I told Steve how I foiled Mr. Chin and Steve earned a new nickname. 'The Ambassador.'

After about an hour or so we decided to pull over at a vacant pristine beach to explore a little. Steve suggested we go for a swim and I agreed. No one was around, so we just dropped our clothes and dove into the water in our undershorts. The water felt great since the cove was fed by a natural stream running down from the mountains. It was shallow, too. I could wade out a hundred yards and still be only chest-deep. I splashed happily, floating with my face toward the sun. After an extended swim, we went back to the car, toweled off and just stood there, marveling at the natural beauty of the place.

"There's nothing around for miles," I said. "Why isn't there a hotel here?"

Upon our return to our own hotel, we struck up a conversation with the concierge, telling him about the cove we discovered.

"Oh yeah, I know that place," he replied. "That little cove has the largest collection of sharks in the islands. They love where the cold water from the stream meets the shallow sea."

Good God. I'd waded out the length of a football field, splashing around like a goof, with only my underwear to protect me. I might as well have had a bloody steak tied around my neck.

After a refreshing weekend we returned to Honolulu and to our hotel. My room was on the 40th floor of a 44-story high-rise. I stuck my keycard in the door, thinking about what a nice weekend it had been. Just as I opened the door, I heard a loud cooing sound. Suddenly chaos erupted as fifty pigeons burst into a wild frenzy, frantically headed for the narrow window I'd left open all weekend. I was picking up feathers for days.

***

I discovered early on in my career that I would do things for a TV show that I would never otherwise do in real life. For example, while working for the government I was shooting a show in England and decided I needed some aerial shots. Today, that is best accomplished by a helicopter or drone with a nose-mounted camera controlled with joysticks. But the only option available to me back then was to go up in a chopper with its doors open and hang out the side.

Let me go on the record that I do not like helicopters. An experienced pilot once told me, "A helicopter is five thousand parts flying in close formation. Never fly higher than you want to fall or farther than you want to walk back."

Steve was shooting from a helicopter once when a red light the size of a bumper sticker lit up the dashboard. The pilot yelled, "We're going down." Fortunately, the pilot managed to auto-rotate the thing down safely, but it landed hard and everyone was pretty shaken up.

I did know of another friend who wasn't so lucky. So, I don't like helicopters. I feel like I'm tempting fate. I only go up when I must.

In England, after emptying my pockets of anything that could fly out and damage the tail rotor, I strapped both myself and the camera to the helicopter with enough lead to reach the open door. Up we went.

Strapped in and ready to hang out the open door. Looking at this photo I'm sure it was the month-long trip in 1994 where we played pool and drank Guinness every single night of the trip. I returned home 30 pounds heavier than when I left.

A helicopter with the door open is extremely noisy and brutally cold. Once we got to the location I stepped out on the edge of the opening. As the wind ripped at my arms I got my shots.

After a few minutes I told the pilot over the headset that I wanted to go to the second location. Instead of gently tapering off toward the west the pilot decided to have a little fun with me and sharply banked. The helicopter was now on its side and I found myself hanging out the open door, looking straight down at a bunch of very tiny cows scattering like ants as the tall grass bent down from the prop wash. The next time I gave the pilot instructions I sat down and strapped into my seat first.

The pilots grin before taking me up to hang like a piñata high above England. Tom Pokorny on the left, me on the right with Ray Kreiner next to me, posing with the RAF crew in England.

I've always felt that I was a lucky guy. I mean, just look at the experiences I've amassed, never even leaving my home town.

It was during a month-long shoot in England (as seen in the photo above) with my friends Tom and Ray that I discovered, although he has many blessings in his life, my friend Tom was not what you'd call a lucky person.

I mean, here was a guy who bought a brand new car and, as he was driving into the dealership with the check in his pocket, the car was smashed and totaled. Only they didn't total it because it was brand new. They repaired it, bent frame and all.

Then there was the time be parked his brand new pickup truck under a tree only to see a storm send a large tree branch crashing through the sunroof.

But in England, I got to witness Tom's misery up close.

As we checked into our first accommodations we were put up in an old manor house. Walking up one flight of stairs we were faced with three doors. I opened my door and saw a living room with a couch and fireplace, a well-appointed kitchen and a separate bedroom.

Ray opened his door to something even more opulent, a living room with a bigger couch and a huge bay window, a nice kitchen and a separate bedroom.

Tom opened his door and the door hit the bed.

And the bed was the size of something you might find on a submarine. They'd mounted the TV to the ceiling as that was the only available space.

Our next stop was a place Ray stayed out before and insisted we lodge there for a week. It had a fine pub downstairs where we could drink Guinness every night while shooting pool, only to retire upstairs. It was the beer at this place and the full English breakfasts that I attribute the 30 pounds I gained during this trip.

At the pub, Ray and I got nice, quiet cozy rooms off the main hallway while Tom's room was up a few steps and down a long narrow corridor.

It was right over the kitchen where the baking staff arrived to clang pots and pans each morning at four.

To make matters worse, Tom's room was built into an eave of the old house. He had to step up into his shower and bend down, facing a shower head that shot hot water directly into his face. Good morning!

But what a great friend he's become over the years. I can't imagine life without him.

***

In February of 1993 I headed for the island of Crete. It was the first leg of a three-week European shooting trip. I was warned before I left to beware of Greek Customs. But I never imagined it would be as tough as it turned out to be.

Due to a tight budget, there would be only two people going on this shoot - me and my aforementioned colleague, Ray Kreiner. Kreiner was an audio guy with a developing talent as a camera operator. I was by now a trusted producer who could shoot and do lighting. Together, we'd have to do it all. Trouble began as soon as we touched Greek soil.

In Athens we claimed our luggage to clear customs before continuing to Crete. We had three large anvil cases of television equipment, two personal suitcases, and two small carry-on bags. The first obstacle we faced was the two of us maneuvering this bulky assortment of unwieldy equipment through the airport.

Clumsily, we deposited ourselves and our pile of belongings in front of the customs desk. Eying me over carefully was Customs Agent #1 (CA 1). CA 1 rapidly asked me a series of questions in Greek, causing me to stare blankly and turn my head slightly to the side, like Nipper the RCA dog that hears his master's voice. Snapping back to reality takes half a second longer after you've just crossed seven time zones.

Fighting through my jet lag I tried to look cooperative. I launched into an impromptu game of Charades, pointing to the luggage and acting out the word "television." We gathered the attention of the other Customs Agents and, looking around, realized that we were the only people in the airport being detained. Soon there were no other passengers in the Arrivals Terminal to divert their distrustful gaze.

Unsure of what she was after, I began convincing Customs Agent #1 that our final destination was Crete, since that seemed like the kind of information she desired. Sternly she indicated for me to wait. CA 1 handed me off to Customs Agent #2, a tall, dark young Greek man. He directed an old man, Customs Agent #3, to wrap up our production gear with blue plastic straps and to clamp them on tightly with metal fasteners. He also affixed large red and white, unreadable Greek language labels all over of our equipment cases.

Hustling us along like unwanted sheep, CA 2 herded us away from the customs desk and out of the terminal. He began hailing a taxi for us. If I understood him correctly, we would all take a short trip somewhere that I would pay for.

I was confused and exasperated. Anything, I thought, to get out of here.

Most of the cabbies slowed down, looked at our pile of gear and continued past us to easier prey. Finally, with the help of a cop, CA 2 wrestled one of the taxi drivers down. The bewildered cabbie looked at the three of us with our luggage and scratched his head. CA 2 yelled at him in Greek and the poor cabbie reluctantly began to load the three large cases into the trunk of his cab.

The most expensive piece of gear, the case with the camera, wound up on top of the pile sticking out of the trunk and the driver secured it with a single, frayed bungee cord. Then Kreiner, Customs Agent

#2 and I and the cabbie climbed into the little cab with our suitcases and carry-ons.

Like a man late for dinner, the cab driver hit the gas and the cases in the trunk lurched and bucked. As we sped around curves toward the airport exit, I shouted "Slow down!" The Greek cabbie might have thought I said, "Hurry up," for all I know. In my mind I imagined the destruction of our forty-five-thousand-dollar camera strewn across an Athens highway before we'd even rolled an inch of tape.

Frantically fingering at the pages of my Greek guide I found the word for slow - αργός - but the cab hit a bump and instead my finger landed on the word Argos, a city that's a two-hour drive from the airport. "Ahh," grinned the customs agent. The cabbie put down the pedal with new contempt.

It turned out our actual destination was a freight terminal where we would ship the containers via air freight to Crete. Hoisting the three 90-pound cases up onto a six-foot-high loading dock, we then wheeled them into the building and into the waiting hands of a shipping agent. And I paid another fifty bucks for them to be shipped to Crete.

We hopped back into the waiting cab and whisked CA 2 back to the International Terminal while Kreiner and I, along with our suitcases, continued on with the cab to the Domestic Air Terminal. It was there that the cabbie performed a careful ballet of extortion.

Straight-faced, he asked me for 80,000 drachmas. The exchange rate was only hours old to me, but I knew something was wrong. Surely, he meant 8,000. But that still seemed like too much. I offered 5,000. He said 80,000 again. I said 5,000, handed it to him and got out of the cab. Reluctantly he accepted the 5,000 then begged for a tip. I gave him another thousand drachmas. We found out later that the correct amount for this trip should have been only one thousand drachmas, fifteen hundred at the most. Welcome to Greece.

After the debacle with Greek Customs taking our gear and being ripped off by the taxi driver we had a considerable layover to wait for the flight to Crete. When we did finally board, the plane was full, hot and smelly. I was pressed up against the window, although I couldn't see anything because it was pitch black dark outside.

The flight finally took off after midnight. Our contact in Crete was due to meet us sometime after 1:00 AM. As the plane approached the island, the wind rocked the plane left and right violently. It was one of those times when I seriously wondered if the plane would be able to land at all and I truly feared for my life. Just before it touched down one big puff of wind rocked the plane to one side and the pilot literally brought it down sideways on one wheel.

After an exhausting full day of traveling I was relieved to see our contact. He led us to our hotel and confirmed that the customs office on Crete was closed until morning. We would have to pick up the gear the next day. In my stupor that suited me fine. Getting through Athens was unusual, but on Crete, the circus began in earnest.

The next morning our first stop was the downtown office of Olympic Air Freight. Finding their tiny, back-alley office was the first challenge. From the freight office's counter, I could see our fragile camera gear through a window lying haphazardly on a broken curb beside a beat-up old black step van. Even though we couldn't yet have it handed over to us, it was comforting to see that it had made it to Crete.

After getting our paperwork signed, we were instructed to follow the step van down to the waterfront office of Greek Customs Crete, a large, filthy warehouse with cars parked tightly inside against the walls. One of the cars was a sleek mid-70's Jaguar XJ6. Like the rest of the automobiles in there, it had a heavy layer of dust on it so thick that the original paint color was indistinguishable. The side window of the Jag had been rubbed clean at some point so a person could peer into its interior. The car had been there so long that the spot on the window had been again covered over with a thick layer of new dust. I silently hoped I had better luck with these customs people than the owner of that Jag.

The van driver motioned for me to go upstairs. From this point on I would be separated for the rest of the morning from Kreiner and our contact.

I was escorted through dusty back offices to sit down at a cluttered little table with Customs Agent #4, a fidgety man who was somewhat hyperactive. I was only going to be in Greece for a few days and I hadn't bothered to study the language. Unfortunately, this guy didn't know my language either.

I handed him my equipment list, a cover letter stating that I was on official business and my signed receipt for the air freight. CA 4 grimaced and shook his head. His questions became another series of Charades. He left the table twice. Each time he returned my scenario seemed to look bleaker.

The third time he left I found myself sitting alone for about twenty minutes. The room was so cold I could see my breath. As I looked around, I noticed that the same dust from the warehouse below had dulled every flat surface in this tiny, squalid office. I rose and stood in the hallway trying to remain patient. Normally I consider myself well-versed enough to talk my way out of situations like this. But in Greece, because of the language barrier, I was practically mute.

After what seemed like an eternity CA 4 returned and had apparently done. He could so he turned me over to Customs Agent #5, a very serious man. His steely, black eyes gazed down at me like the sheriff who, after a ten-year search, had finally captured the serial killer. He was a big man and, due to the coldness of the room, wore a big maroon winter coat that made him look even bigger. Cigarette smoke steamed through his clenched teeth as he beckoned me to follow him.

We sat down at his desk. Slowly and methodically, he generated a four-page official Greek customs document that included my equipment list. My list was stapled onto the document and an official-looking stamp was put across the edges of paper where the equipment list met the rest of the form. CA 5 spoke just a little English, but we still had a lot of difficulty communicating.

He was very concerned with exactly when I was leaving Greece. He fought hard to be clear that the date of my departure was very important for some reason. He totaled up the value of my equipment in US dollars: $75,000. This seemed important to him. "Very expensive," he said.

As he asked me another series of questions, I began to wonder what my friends downstairs were doing. Hours were passing and they had no idea where I was. While my mind wandered, CA 5 asked Customs Agent #6 across the room a series of questions in Greek. I knew that they were talking about me, but I had no idea what they were saying. Points were being argued and seemingly important decisions were made. I understood none of it.

My focus fell to my body language and I tried to look friendly and cooperative. CA 5 took the documents across the room to Customs Agent #7, who put a few more official stamps on them before Customs Agent #8 initialed them.

CA 5 returned and asked for my passport. I stood, put my foot on the chair and rolled up my pants leg. Taking the passport out of the money belt velcroed to my leg, I handed it over to him. He wrote a lengthy note in my passport that, to the best of my understanding, meant I was responsible for twelve million drachmas worth of television equipment.

CA 5 painstakingly xeroxed everything, including my passport. He then walked me down the hall and introduced me to the Assistant Director, a short, scrappy well-dressed woman with fire in her eyes.

She reluctantly signed my documents. Then the three of us went in to see the Director, an old man with the only decent office in the building.

As we entered CA 5 cautioned me to treat the Director with respect. The Director asked CA 5 a few questions in Greek then signed my document and waved his hand at me as a get-out-of-my-office type of gesture. Bending and scraping in thanks, I tried to leave. Instead the Assistant Director physically cornered me. She picked up my documents off the Director's desk, got right up in my face and waved them under my nose.

"You must turn this in to Customs at the airport in Athens when you leave Greece. Do you understand? You must turn this document in to Customs when you leave!" she shouted. "If you don't, we will come and find you at..." she looked down at the paperwork... "Baltimore. We will find you."

She stared me in the eyes. Her face was barely an inch from mine. I can still see the broken blood vessels in her eyes. She was putting on a show for the Director.

I was impressed.

The Director was not.

Finally breaking off, she motioned to CA 5 and said something along the lines of "Get him out of here."

Finally, reunited downstairs with my friends, they were exasperated. They had no idea where I'd been for the last four hours. CA 5 led me past them to see Customs Agent #9, who took my air freight receipt. He wrote up a new receipt, asking me to pay him another 3,000 drachmas. On top of this he whispered he wanted another 200 drachmas for "the stamp." The extra 200 was not on the receipt and clearly a shakedown but I gave it to him to avoid the hassle of another argument. I felt too close to leaving.

We all trampled back down the dusty, ramshackle stairs to the ground floor. We had to travel down one person at a time because the steps were so old they swayed on the verge of collapse.

Back in the squalid warehouse, my equipment cases were opened and inspected. A tenth customs agent surveyed this operation and he asked to see the first item on my equipment list. It was the front end of the Betacam camera, complete with serial number. That's when it hit me. I had made a terrible mistake.

I was lazy before I left and I had brought a colleague's equipment list and not generated one myself. I felt these lists were a nuisance and never actually used. What would be the harm of taking someone else's list? I was relieved when the serial numbers matched. Thank God I had taken the same camera as the guy whose equipment list I'd borrowed. CA 10 was satisfied with this test, and we were finally able to leave with our equipment.

The ordeal at the customs house had taken half a day. The loss of time threw our shoot schedule into a tailspin but Kreiner and I were able to complete two days' worth of work in a day and a half. It was a relief to finally get something on tape. Caught up with the shoot, I hadn't yet realized just how big a mistake I had made.

After two short days, it was time to leave Crete. We planned to depart very early on a Saturday morning. The cases still bore the bold stickers that the customs officials in Athens had plastered all over them. As Kreiner and I wheeled our belongings out of the hotel and toward the car for the airport, I paused a moment to ask our hotel manager if he could tell me exactly what the stickers translated out to read.

"Warning: Items Subject to Greek Customs Control and Search," he said.

I whispered to Kreiner, "Well, we're not stuck in customs anymore.

I'm going to rip these stickers off."

"You'd better not do that," he said, cautioning me against the wrath of authority.

One of the actual stickers Greek Customs slapped on my gear.

He looked worried. Figuring that we were flying only to Athens and staying overnight there and that the stickers may confuse the domestic airline baggage handlers, I ripped them off. Just to be safe, I saved them, so I could put them back on later if necessary.

Trying to decipher the Greek language on Crete. This was a rest room.

Everything went well in Athens. We claimed our luggage, stored it in the hotel and had a nice day touring the city, save the fact Kreiner lost his wallet in a taxi and it took us the rest of the day to find it.

Early the next morning we were scheduled to leave Greece. As I dressed for the airport I finally realized just how big a mistake I made.

The Official Greek Customs Document that I helped to generate supposedly contained all the items that I had brought into Greece. Thinking back on it, Customs' concern must have been that I would sell the gear on the black market and avoid taxes. The Customs people were adamant that I take everything back out of Greece that I brought in or pay heavy fines. The bogus list was now a part of an official Greek customs document.

I reached into my bag, pulled out the document and looked at the list inside. My fears were confirmed. The list contained at least six items that I had not brought with me: a tripod, a color monitor, monitor batteries, a charger, and some other things. If a customs official asked to see any of these items I could not produce them. The official document that I helped to create said that I had brought them all in to Greece. Now I would have to prove I'm taking them all out. I couldn't because I never really brought them in.

I knew that the customs people probably didn't know a monitor battery from a camera battery, but this list was very carefully put together. Each of the items were listed and numbered. What worried me the most was the color monitor. It had a serial number on it. If asked about it there was no way I could produce that. I took a deep breath and thought about my dilemma as dawn was cresting outside my window. My heart sank. Exactly how was I going to get out of this?

I tried to be rational. As far as I could see, there were two possible scenarios. I didn't like either of them.

Scenario One: I could alter the Official Greek Customs Document to accurately reflect the things in my equipment package. I could just scratch things off the list. This would be a bad idea because seeing items scratched off the list would look suspicious. The last thing I wanted was to look suspicious. I wasn't even thinking that they had made xerox copies of everything. If I didn't like scenario one, I hated number two.

Scenario Two: I could just hand over the list and hope the customs officials at the airport were lazy. This was not a comforting option. If caught, it would look like I was trying to pull a fast one. I knew that if it came to me having to explain the situation, I was sunk. I already had a lot of difficulty communicating with the Greeks. And banking on them being lazy was not likely considering they had been so methodical letting us into the country.

Customs people don't like games. My throat turned to chalk and my stomach knotted. A chill shot through me and I noticed my hand was shaking. With time running out and no other options coming to mind, I decided to go with Scenario Two: bank on the laziness.

My mind filled with possibilities.

I had visions of being handcuffed and taken to jail because I didn't have the money to pay import tariffs on the missing items.

I would have to call the American embassy.

I envisioned Kreiner getting on the plane that I would be unable to board.

Our equipment would be confiscated. The whole rest of the European shoot would be blown.

I recalled tales of Greek prisons where they don't feed the inmates. They expect the inmate's family to provide them with food. My family was 5,000 miles away.

Greek prison. If an inmate is going to poke you in the brown eye and stir your peanut butter you can sure bet, it'll be in a Greek prison.

I have no desire to dance the chocolate cha cha while some woolly bully is yanking the pulley.

If some Hellenic Hells Angel wants to blow the rusty trombone I don't want to be in his orchestra.

Fuck if I'm biting the pillow for Uncle Sam. How did I get into this?

A shitstorm was brewing and there was no one to blame but me. I had so many details to deal with before this trip. Could it be that I'd be sodomized by something as mundane as an equipment list?

Who I could turn to for help? To my knowledge Kreiner had no clue what was going on. I could fill him in but that might upset him as much as it did me. I decided not to tell him. I wanted him to look perfectly unnerved in front of the customs people and, if memory served well, he could not act anyway.

I carefully selected my clothes that morning, ones that would be durable for prison.

When I met Kreiner at the hotel checkout, I didn't know if he noticed that I was preoccupied in thought. We took a cab to the airport in silence. Upon arrival the two of us shoved the three large anvil cases, our two suitcases and two carry-on bags up to the ticketing area. The ticket agent was all ready to check our bags through without question. Then the image of the Assistant Director threatening me came back into my head. I looked at Kreiner and, shrugging my shoulders, I opened my bag and gave the ticket agent the official Greek Customs Document. He looked at it carefully. His face drew long. Then he picked up the telephone. Cupping the receiver, he grew solemn.

"You must leave this building. Take your bags down to the Arrivals Terminal. The customs officials will meet you there."

He handed the document back to me while pointing us back toward the door. I glanced at Kreiner. He had that `What is this bullshit?' look on his face.

Once again, we gathered up our voluminous belongings and shoved them back out into the chilly morning. Traveling with production gear is a very unglamorous part of television. By the look on Kreiner's face, he was starting to get tired of the hassle. But my mind was far away. "Please don't look carefully at these bags," was all I could think.

The walk to the next building was not a long one but for me it felt like it took a lifetime.

Kreiner looked relaxed and carefree at the airport, unaware of the situation.

The automatic doors of the Arrivals Terminal swooshed open like the jaws of the valley of death. We pushed our bags inside.

A big, beefy woman with wiry black hair came around a corner to meet us. She was the 11th customs official I would deal with on this trip. Customs Agent #11 had a demeanor that suggested we had imposed upon her nap time; however, now that she was awake, she would make us pay for that transgression.

CA 11 quickly took charge. She gestured for us to lay the cases down flat. Reluctantly, I handed her the Official Greek Customs Document, the one that said I should have things that I did not possess. Taking a firm hold of the document, she eyed it carefully. My throat was as dry as an old dog bone in the summer sun. I looked at Kreiner. He had lit a cigarette and stood there as cool as a man could be. Thank God for that.

CA 11 drew her finger down the equipment list. At random, she pointed to an item. "Show me this," she said.

Anxiously I looked at the list where she was pointing. She had picked out the back end of the Betacam camera. I unlocked the case. Pulling it out, I knew that we had checked the front end earlier and the numbers matched, but I had no idea if the back end would. We had recently been experimenting with different camera parts. "Please, God, let the serial number be right," I prayed as I searched for the elusive number.

There it was. It matched.

"What is in the other two cases?" she asked.

Kreiner smoothly opened one of the cases with one hand, his cigarette curling up smoke around his face. Meanwhile I desperately tore at the clasps of the second case, my heart pounding through my chest. Looking into one of the open cases, she asked to see into the audio bag. Kreiner opened it for her. She nodded. She looked at

Kreiner's face. He was just another perturbed passenger dealing with an inquisitive customs agent. In short, he looked fine. She looked down into my case and eyed the equipment list again. "Is this everything?" she asked.

Kreiner and I nodded that it was. She glanced over the document again then looked me straight in the eye. At that moment, I stopped breathing. But I lived what my father taught me. If you don't know what you're doing at least look like you know what you're doing. I forced a smile. And I didn't blink. She looked tired, weary. "Wait here," she said, walking into a little room.

We waited for fifteen long minutes during which time my mind flooded with possibilities.

"Could it be that we managed to get through customs?"

"Were they waiting for someone else to rummage through our things?"

"Would a bang bro in Block B bank a blind broner in my backyard?"

Finally, yet another official, Customs Agent #12, showed up. The official document was not in his hand. CA 12 asked us to follow him with our gear. He escorted us and our equipment back to the ticket counter where he watched our bags be loaded onto the airline's conveyor belt. Then he turned on his heel and left. When he walked through the door I finally managed to breathe again.

We were on our way out of Greece.

As I boarded the plane the relief I felt was immeasurable. Compared to Greece, the rest of our European trip was a breeze. Upon landing in Germany, we walked through customs with barely a nod. Once outside the terminal I collapsed to my knees and kissed the ground. Kreiner looked at me like I was crazy. "Tonight, over a beer, I'll tell you what really happened back there," I said.

It was a stupid mistake on my part and I was lucky to get out of Greece. I've never gone back.

Telling Kreiner the whole story over a small beer in Germany.

***

It's a warm Saturday morning in Berlin. The sun is still low and the shadows are long. I'm sitting outside at a communal table with a hot latte and ciabatta sandwich. Most of the restaurants in Berlin provide blankets for patrons to use in cool weather but I don't see one. I bang the table with my chair and apologize in English, not wanting to offend the two local men dressed in black sharing the small table. Neither responds. Sitting down I notice an electrical box in front of me, peeling with layers of promotional posters, each vying to get an audience for an event.

A box covered in layers of promotional posters in Berlin.

Across the street a construction crane stands silently above the intersection. As a young woman glides by on a bicycle with a red cello case strapped to her back I think about the crane. If they construct a building taller than the six-story building currently on that corner the morning sun will no longer bathe this corner like it does this morning and that would be a shame. My illuminated sidewalk is crowded with interesting looking people. Ten well-dressed young men walk by and all but one has an eye opener - an open beer. It is only seven o'clock in the morning. No one cares. This is Berlin.

Finishing their small coffees and cigarettes the two men at my table rise to leave at the same time but it is obvious they are not together. One leaves his coffee cup on the table and hops on a bike while the other takes his white porcelain cup and saucer back inside. Seeing this the cyclist dismounts and carries his own cup inside too. He doesn't seem to know the custom. I watch him react. Perhaps he thinks I am the local.

Under my feet I feel the faint vibrations of the U-Bahn far below. It stirs me like a soft alarm. It's time to get back to work.

***

On February 5th, 1995 at approximately 3:45 PM, I was thirty five and still working at NSA. It was a snow day and I had the day off. For me, the time, the place and the situation is frozen in time as it was a moment that nearly changed my life.

I was lying on an old-fashioned metal sled. My little boy Graham jumped on my back and we flew down a steep snow-covered hill. Setting off from the top Graham and I quickly picked up some serious speed. Immediately I realized that, not only could I not slow down, but I could not steer either, as nearly a foot of snow had fallen and we were stuck in a deep channel, packed down firm where another sledder had gone before us. Soon, we were out of control and on a collision course with that same sledder - a man now standing at the bottom of the hill, the only other sledder at Oregon Ridge on this barren, winter Sunday. He is there with his own son, a boy almost the same age as Graham. Off near the parking lot his wife is chatting with my wife. But I know this man is not an ordinary sledder. I recognized him - even said hello to him earlier when my son and I began our ascent to the top of the hill. This other sledder and I are the same age, born only a few months apart, yet our lives could not be more different.

For the other sledder is Baltimore's star shortstop Cal Ripken, Jr. He's known as The Iron Man. He had played every single game for the Baltimore Orioles *for the last twelve years*. He was chasing a record - a record that stood for over half a century. A record so rare that many said it would never be broken. Until Cal Ripken came along, no one had even come within 5 years of breaking Lou Gehrig's record of playing in 2,130 consecutive major league baseball games. And, even though Ripken had played in every game since 1982, even he had not quite broken it yet. On this day he is only a mere 122 games away from the most revered record in sports and was on pace to break the record that coming season.

That is, *if* he avoids injury.

This ride was my son's first time on a sled. Too young to go sledding the year before, now two and a half Graham was excited by the prospect. It had been an unusually warm winter thus far, but February 5th brought the first major snowstorm, dumping a foot of fresh powder on Baltimore County. I selected Oregon Ridge for his first sledding experience, in retrospect a poor choice. A one-hundred-and-forty-foot peak with a sharp incline, Oregon Ridge is an abandoned ski slope and the equivalent of sledding straight down from the height of a twelve-story building. I've subsequently learned that others had been clocked at fifty miles per hour on this hill. And now my two-year-old son is desperately clinging to my back as we fly down from the summit. Cal Ripken does not see me, my son, or the sled.

As we flew down the hill, gaining speed and unable to steer, the magnitude of the situation slowly dawned upon me and unfolded like a movie in slow motion. Images begin to flash through my mind.

Bill Buckner lets the ball pass through his legs in the 1986 World Series.

Scott Norwood misses a thirty-six-yard kick to lose the 1991 Super

Bowl.

In the passionate world of sports, these are very bad moments indeed. If I injured Cal Ripken - if I personally hurt the Iron Man - if my sledding accident somehow contributed to the end of "the streak" - I would be a pariah. No matter who I became, no matter what I accomplished, no matter what I did with my life, that's all I'd ever be known for. A very bad thing indeed. Yet, here I am, *we are* – me and my innocent fresh-faced son on his first sledding ride - hurtling toward infamy.

The press would be relentless with this story. Not only was this no ordinary achievement Cal Ripken was on the verge of obtaining, this was no ordinary off-season for baseball. America's pastime had suffered a horrible blow the past year as a bitter strike led to an eight-month work stoppage and the cancellation of the World Series, the first cancelation in nearly a century. Even World War II didn't stop the World Series - yet they canceled it in 1994 due to a greedy, ugly strike. The great American game now needed a boost – one great story – something good to bring back the fans. That story would be Cal Ripken and the streak. He was the workingman's hero. He was someone the average American could identify with. He was that guy who showed up every day and just did his job. He is also the guy who still does not see me as I rocket towards him on an out of control sled with a two-year-old on my back at fifty miles per hour.

"Get outta the way!" I scream but he does not hear me.

I rip and tug at the sled's handles, back and forth, but I cannot steer out of this deep tract.

"Cal -Aaghhh!" I scream, to no reaction.

He has his padded hood up, a drawstring pulling it tightly to his ears. His dark blue one-piece nylon snowsuit is getting bigger and bigger as we head straight for his right Achilles tendon. The man who has not

156

taken a sick day since May 30th, 1982 will not move out of my way and I cannot avoid him. It is only two months before the start of the baseball season and I am about to hit him hard and fast with a blindsided blow. I think I am going to crush his ankle.

I have only a split second to decide before we are upon him. As we approach his unsuspecting legs I roll out to my right, upending the sled while shouting,

"Hold on, Graham - we need to take one for the team!"

Narrowly missing Ripken, the sled plowed to a stop as I slid head first into deep snow. Graham held onto my coat with his little hands until his thirty-pound body was catapulted airborne Superman style into the soft virgin snow beyond. Blinded by a face full of snow, I scrambled to my feet and raced toward my son, a little puffball in a red hat about six feet away.

Pulling him out of the drift, I saw his frost-covered face belie a toothy grin that said,

"Let's do that again, Daddy."

Years later, when Graham was a teenager, he and I climbed back to the top of Oregon Ridge to go sledding and we recalled the story of Cal Ripken and the near miss. Graham speculated,

"What do you think would've happened had we hit Cal Ripken that day?"

I said, "What do you think?"

Graham responded, "Well, maybe he would've befriended us, died of his injuries and left us all his money."

I said, "It's more like we would been driven out of the country, our family hounded and our names dragged through history as 'The Streak Killers.'"

The real way it ended was quietly, that afternoon so long ago on a cold winter's day during baseball's 1995 off season. Sitting in the soft new snow, my eyes closed, holding little Graham closely, relieved that he was safe, chastising myself for taking a two-year-old boy down such a steep hill, we rocked quietly together celebrating the safe successful conclusion of his first sled ride. Then I opened my eyes and squinted to see the looming, six-foot four, silent figure before us. Yes, there he stood - unscathed – his hood still pulled up tightly, framing his famous face - a man who, in seven months and a day, would tip his cap to the world in a stadium full of deafening cheers for on September 6th, after the top of the fifth inning, when it became official that he had played in his 2,131st consecutive game, a capacity crowd including both the President and the Vice President of the United States would stand and cheer and not stop cheering for well over ten minutes. Fireworks would explode, the world would watch on TV and every other baseball game would stop for a moment as Cal Ripken takes a victory lap around Oriole Park at Camden Yards, breaking the record and credited with saving baseball in the process. In a time of high-priced athletes, bad behavior, free agents and over indulgences, one humble hard-working ball player, a solid role model, a guy who stayed and played with his hometown team and one of the rare good guys, takes his bow and in the process, gives us all one bright and shining moment in the history of sports.

But none of that had happened yet. There he stood, a few feet away, no cheering crowd, just a silent, lone silhouette in an all-white landscape standing with his small son. I'd only missed hitting him by about three inches but that was all it took. I don't even know if the great man realized just how close we came. We watched as he glanced over at us and our upended sled and saw that we were OK. I could just make out a faint smile as it crossed his face then his blue eyes narrowed and it was time for him to leave, his rare solitude with his boy interrupted. With a slight nod to us, his back straightened, he spun off his left, tugged on the yellow nylon rope of his sled, took his little boy's hand and trudged off toward the parking lot, the February silence broken only by his heavy boots crunching through the newly fallen snow. I whispered softly to Graham,

"There goes Cal Ripken, off to meet his appointment with destiny."

***

It is another February and decades have passed since avoiding Cal Ripken. My boy and his beautiful little sister have grown. I am not a famous baseball player. Just Jeff Dugan. An obscure television producer. But life has been good.

Wandering through Berlin's Pergamon Museum I walk up the steps of the Pergamon altar, painstakingly rebuilt here, brick by brick from its excavation site. I am in awe of the gigantic Market Gate of Miletus and walk through its arches like weary travelers did thousands of years earlier. I examine the Ishtar Gate with wonderment and am humbled by the sheer scale of these magnificent archeological pieces. These are the scattered remnants of a nearly forgotten civilization. The words of Dr. Melissa Hilbish, a teacher from Johns Hopkins, echo in my head as I reflexively question who decides what goes into a museum and why. I pause to consider the collective memories of Pergamon and think of all those people and their personal memories and how they are all but forgotten. There must have been so many. Now they are nameless and faceless, like grains of sand on a beach.

On this day in February the Catholic Church celebrates Ash Wednesday and I hear the echoes of the priests of my youth,

"Remember man that you are dust, and unto dust you shall return."

I think of the things I've created and how fragile the stuff of this life really is.

On October 5th, 1995 I had the attention of viewers all over the world, if only for a moment.

***

I had worked as a freelance camera operator for the international Catholic cable network EWTN for a few years when I learned that Pope John Paul II was coming to the US. They needed a producer to coordinate coverage of his North American tour. Somehow, I convinced them I was just the man for the job.

My camera operator for this adventure would be my good friend Larry. He and I had joined the Pope Tour the day before in Newark, New Jersey, where Pope John Paul II was received by President Clinton. An estimated 1,000 journalists were tracking his visit along with us. Giants Stadium was setting a new attendance record with nearly 83,000 people packed into the place. We were stationed in a ratty old press box, a literal dump of abused wood and metal with a single ancient phone sitting on the window ledge, a tattered remnant of countless sporting events. In fact, all of old Giants Stadium was a dump. They hadn't even bothered to cover up the billboards for the Pope's visit. There was an enormous Budweiser sign right next to the big screen where the Pope would appear. I could almost hear a faint play by play announcer...

"It's the King of Kings... brought to you by... the King of Beers, Budweiser. After the Mass, settle down to the smooth taste of a nice, cold Budweiser. I confess - this Bud's for you!"

Mark Zimmerman, Larry Bowers and me in the booth at Giants Stadium.

In the fetid press box stood Jeff Burson, the engineer for EWTN, and a fresh-faced field reporter named Mark Zimmerman. I knew Burson was a real pro and by the time Larry and I had arrived all the cables had been run, the camera was set up and everything had been technically checked out, waiting for us. The plan was to record to a remote truck outside while simultaneously beaming up to a satellite for live network coverage. As the on-site producer, it was my job to line up some interviews for Mark and then just make sure everything was OK when the Pope arrived. I poked my head into the hall and spotted New Jersey Governor Christie Todd Whitman and quickly dragged her into our skybox. She was very sharp, and Mark did a good interview with her.

Elated after a coup with the Governor, we all breathed easily, kicked back and waited for the Pope. The day before, we had snagged an exclusive interview with New York Mayor Rudy Giuliani and the network was very happy with the footage I'd sent. Nothing to do now but wait for the Man in the Big Hat. As time passed, Larry noticed that the camera was running off batteries. Not wanting to take any chances, Larry asked Burson if we had any extra batteries. Burson told Larry that there were some on the charger down in the truck. Larry asked me if we had any idea about the Pope's arrival time. I didn't since the Secret Service was hush-hush about the details. The crowd outside looked docile, sitting patiently in a steady rain. Then Larry asked if I thought it'd be OK if he ran down and retrieved some spares. My mind drifted back to the time I was shooting winter sailboat racing for *Evening Magazine* where I'd taken every one of their crap batteries out on the boat, only to have them fail, one by one, before the end of the race. I looked back out at the docile crowd and said, "Go for it."

Mark, Burson and I waited and waited. No Larry. Burson had a walkie-talkie and radioed down to the truck. He learned from the truck engineer that Larry had been stopped on his way back up by the Secret Service because his credentials somehow were not in order. We all had a stack of credentials on a chain around our neck as the Secret Service would issue specific ones for each little event during the week – then change them at some point in an attempt to stay ahead of potential forgers. The result was more like a confused assault on the real press who were constantly trying to disseminate the changes down through the ranks of each network. Burson told me he'd straighten it out and shot out of the press box carrying his walkie-talkie. I sat down and looked at Mark sitting silently across from me. I saw fear in his eyes. Suddenly I felt like I was on my own during the silent seconds before a perfect storm. I didn't have long to ponder.

BBRRRRRRIIINNNGGG!! Suddenly the ancient phone on the ledge burst to life. I picked it up. It was EWTN Headquarters in Alabama.

"The Pope's coming!"

"What?! Now?"

"Yep. Right now. He'll be coming into the far gate by the   big speaker column. He'll be in the Popemobile. He'll circle the outer ring of the stadium once before heading to the altar. Get on that camera!"

Just at that moment, the capacity crowd stirred to life in a deafening roar. I dropped the phone and leapt onto the camera, haphazardly pointing it at the gate. Let me put this moment into a little perspective. I am a professional camera operator but when you're working off a production truck, the camera is often 'built' for you by the engineer prior to your arrival, which means the parts have been assembled. It is up to the camera operator to spend five minutes making small key adjustments, so the camera is assembled in a way that is comfortable, reliable and familiar.

The first thing is, make sure the camera is balanced so when you release the tilt lock, the camera doesn't want to take a nose dive forward or unnaturally tilt up toward the sky. Next, you ball it out by releasing the head lock under the camera head, making sure the little bubble is level, so it doesn't look like the horizon is crooked creating an inadvertent Dutch Tilt. Then you make minor adjustments to the tilt and pan friction, so the camera smoothly tilts at a forty-five-degree angle without wanting to favor the tilt or pan or, God forbid, one of them is locked down like the time I was totally unprepared and panned the crowd during a live hockey game for a New York station making it look like a major earthquake had just hit the East Coast. Next move the pan handle so the handle doesn't interfere with any possible moves and then make sure the remote zoom attached to the pan handle exactly where the operator can reach for it without looking at it. Also, don't forget to make sure the viewfinder is adjusted in just the right place, so the camera operator can see it because every step is crucial to help ensure that when you're live on the air, the movements look smooth and fluid.

Of course, I'd done none of that.

Larry was working this camera and he'd set it up for himself. The instant I dropped the phone, leapt to the camera and pointed it at the gate, the gate sprang open and the Pope entered the stadium. Simultaneously my tally light came on in the viewfinder indicating that my camera was live on the air. To make things worse, I was zoomed all the way in so every little move I made would be magnified tenfold. I was wrestling to keep the Pope in focus as the little Popemobile circled the stadium when I heard someone screaming on the phone that I'd dropped on the floor. Mark picked it up and held it to my ear. I heard the network guy yelling,

"It's great! It's great! Keep it up. By the way, this is the only camera getting out of the stadium right now. Everybody's taking this shot, Dude. *You're the pool feed for the world!*"

All my career, I had always wanted to have the one shot everyone wanted – to have that one great opportunity, to be in the right place at the right time at least once in my life. Do they give an award for best unprepared camera work? When you frame a close-up of a Pope, do you always keep the entire big hat, or mitre, in the shot? As I panned the camera following the Pope I said a silent prayer that the shot just looked good and everything was crisp and smooth. And I threw in an extra little prayer to that Pope as he drove around in the little lens in front of my right eye:

"Dear Pope, if I ever get another chance in my life to be the pool feed for the world, could I at least have a ten second head's up?"

As the Pope exited the Popemobile and walked up to the altar, I heard on the phone,

"OK, the other networks are up, we're taking the house feed. You're off the hook – good job!" and the tally light on my camera went out.

I slumped back into a chair, glowing with amazement and adrenaline when the door to the press box swung open. In walked Larry holding two batteries. He took one look at me and said, "Did anything happen while I was gone?"

The next day found us at another Mass with 75,000 of the faithful at Aqueduct Racetrack in Queens. This time the Secret Service took a different stance – they kept us *all* out. We had a string of credentials, but they accept none of them. We even had a little area cordoned off for us up next to the altar, but I can't describe it because I never saw it. If there were really 75,000 people there, at least 40,000 were cops with the wrong information about our credentials. That day, at least half of the working media were shut out of the event.

As the producer it fell to me to come up with some form of Plan B. We were taking a pool feed of the Mass, but Mark still needed to do some stand-ups. A stand-up is just that - the reporter stands in front of the camera and talks to the viewers. The plan had been for Mark to do his stand-ups at a little spot in front of the altar right before the Mass, but we were almost out of time since we'd spent so much effort arguing with security. We were barred from entering the mass.

Now we were in an ugly parking lot, pinned next to the satellite truck by a mob trying to get past us. The network needed Mark's live report from Aqueduct within the next minute. I looked at the parking lot. I looked at Mark standing there. What to do?

"Maybe I can climb up on top of the truck and see if I can see anything over the fence," Mark suggested.

Before I could react, Mark scrambled to the top using the tiny metal footholds that folded down off the back of the truck. Now filthy, Mark dusted himself off, ducked under the six-foot-wide satellite dish and peered out into the racetrack.

"I can see the altar, but it's far away," Mark relayed.

"OK, what say you scramble up on top of the uplink truck and get us a shot, Larry?" I pleaded.

We both knew the danger if he did that. It takes a lot of power to send a signal 20 thousand miles into the sky and the satellite dish on an uplink truck puts out a lot of microwave radiation, the kind that cooks a person from the inside out. If he stood in the wrong spot he'd get fried. But the one thing about Larry is he always got the shot. He scrambled onto the top of the truck. When our reporter mentioned the atmosphere was so exciting it felt like there was electricity in the air I hoped he wasn't being sterilized by microwaves.

Then the Mass took place. That is, I assume it took place. All we saw was the parking lot. Mark had to do another live stand up after the Mass and we looked around for something else for him to do. It was still just a dusty parking lot. But when the Mass was over, crowds swarmed into the parking lot and I told Mark to get down right in the middle of the throng and interview the faithful. Soon Mark was surrounded by people and it was captivating. He interviewed about five people and you could tell they were all sincerely moved from the powerful Mass with the Pope. All in all, I think it turned out better than if we'd gotten inside. But our success was fleeting as our only reward was to hustle off to the next chaotic event via a non-glamorous traffic-filled bus ride to Yonkers.

That afternoon we bounded off the bus, racing onto the crowded grounds and joining the Vatican Press Group at St. Joseph's Seminary to be swiftly escorted to our position by security. The timing was so tight that we literally plugged in the camera, microphone and earpiece and we were live on the air within 15 seconds. It was also the place where I'd get as physically close to Pope John Paul II as I ever would since he cruised right past me, only a mere ten feet away. Bam – an hour bus ride for a ten-second shot.

This was as close as I would get to Pope John Paul II during the week we chased him and his entourage all over the east coast of the US in 1995.

Larry gets the shot with only seconds to spare.

This snapshot is my proof that I was actually that close to the Pope. Later Larry, a devout Catholic, would get even closer. Larry was in a receiving line where the Pope shook hands. With the camera still rolling on his right shoulder Larry slowly extended his left hand to get Pope John Paul II to touch it only to feel a Secret Service agent gently pull his arm back by tugging at his elbow from behind.

Then it was back to Manhattan for the next day's Mass in front of 150,000 people in Central Park.

With no rest and a beat-up crew, the moment the Pope left Central Park we packed up and hit the road for another four-hour bus trip back to Baltimore and another Mass the following morning at Oriole Park at Camden Yards. Only one more day of this insane schedule and the Pope would fly back to Rome - and I could get more than four hours of sleep. But as the production van sped down the New Jersey Turnpike toward my hometown, little did I know that my biggest challenge of the Pope Tour was yet to come.

The next morning at dawn Baltimore was eerily quiet. The crew and

I had to take the light rail train into the city as cars were banned. The city was in a total lockdown. Virtually all the downtown streets were closed off to traffic. So, with no other choice, Larry, Mark and I took the Light Rail train into the city, along with hundreds of thousands of others.

Throughout the day, the excitement built as an estimated 350,000 people jammed the Pope's parade route, waiting for a glimpse of the Holy Father as he approached Camden Yards. We showed up at the ball park and found out we were assigned a skybox right behind home plate with a perfect view; literally the best seats in the house.

Baltimore had done it up right. The city covered up all the ball park's advertisements. When the festivities began, a parade of flags from 100 nations was followed by a large group of children in choreographed dance, followed by a high energy gospel choir. The pageantry on display was ten times better than any other event on the Pope's Tour. I mentioned that to Channel 2 anchorwoman Mary Beth Marsden and she quoted me on the air during the local coverage.

The most traveled Pope in history was on his way to my native soil. This visit would mark the first time any Pope had ever visited Baltimore, Maryland - historically known as the birthplace of Catholicism in America. The crowd inside the ball park erupted in cheers when images of the Pope's approaching motorcade flashed up on the huge video screens at Camden Yards. It started to get surreal when forty trumpeters blasted out the theme to 2001: A Space Odyssey as the pope's bullet-proof Mercedes Benz passed Baltimore's World Trade Center.

When he finally arrived at the stadium, Pope John Paul II did a familiar circle around the ball park in his Popemobile. Unlike his appearance at Giants Stadium where I jumped on a camera at the last minute, this time I just sat and watched as my good buddy Larry was safely behind the lens. The sun-drenched Baltimore crowd waved colored flags – red in the upper deck, white at the club level and gold nearer the field - and it was a beautiful sight. Mass began with another fanfare of trumpets and the Pope kissed the altar, surrounded by the deep green grass of Oriole Park. We shot all our necessary footage and the production went perfectly. When the event was over, it felt like Baltimore had been the location of something truly special during this Papal visit. But I had only a moment to soak up the feeling though before Larry, Mark and I had to overcome the biggest hurdle of all and make it to the last of our stops on the Pope Tour.

After the Pope drove out of the ballpark we filed out of the stadium along with 50,000 other people. The Pope's itinerary had him making a brief pit stop at a local soup kitchen then it was off to the airport where he was to be met by Vice President Al Gore before boarding a chartered TWA flight bound for Rome. We had to cover his airport departure and needed to get out to BWI airport as quickly as possible, a trip that normally takes about twenty minutes by car.

I turned the corner and saw that the line for the Light Rail was already three blocks long and building. Once again it was time for the producer's best friend: Plan B.

I turned to Larry.

"There's no way we can take the Light Rail. We'll never make it. We need to find a cab. You guys go to the Holiday Inn. I'll go to the Hyatt. First one to get a cab picks up the others. We have no time – run!"

We split up and I ran the four blocks up to the Hyatt. I huffed and puffed as I stood in front of the hotel for a few minutes catching my breath. I did not see a single car anywhere much less a cab. I put my hands on my knees in utter exhaustion. Then I paced back and forth. I called Larry on his cell phone. He also was having no luck. There simply weren't *any* vehicles on the street. I sank onto the sidewalk and sat in despair.

Then I saw a single vehicle turn off Charles Street and toward the Hyatt. It was an old, beat up taxi with no hubcaps. As it pulled up in front of the Hyatt two guys jumped out and yelled at the cabbie,

"Wait right here – we'll be right back!"

After the two men shot into the hotel I stood up, dusted myself off and calmly strolled over to the cab, speaking to the driver through the open cab window.

"Nice day, huh?" I said.

"Yes. Beautiful day," he answered.

"Say, what do you think the odds are of me getting a cab?"

"I'd say none. The whole city is shut down. No cabs runnin'."

I glanced around and nodded in agreement.

"So, who are those guys?" I asked, gesturing with my thumb toward the hotel.

"They're from CBS," the cabbie said. "They're on their way to the airport."

Again, I nodded. I began to think. Those CBS guys looked tough. I didn't think I stood a good chance of asking them if we could share a ride. After all, there were three of us, two of them, our gear, their luggage... I looked off and saw only the silent street.

"No cabs in the whole city and they left you here all alone, huh?"

"They sure did," he said.

Hmmm. The first rule in television is: just get the shot. Besides, it's always better to ask for forgiveness than permission. I looked at the cabbie again and spoke.

"I'll tell you what. How about I pay what they owe you but instead you take me and my friends to the airport. I'll pay our fare, too – plus, there's an extra fifty in it for you. What do you say?"

The cabbie looked at me unblinking and calmly said, "Your cab has arrived."

I hopped in the cab and we sped off. With no cars on the street but us we quickly made it to the Holiday Inn, picked up Mark and Larry and shot out to the airport. Shortly afterwards, the Pope arrived and Al Gore shook his hand. The Pope finally said his goodbyes to America, stepped onto the plane, and the jet turned into a tiny speck in the darkening sky. I'd done it. I'd jumped over all the hurdles, taken good care of my crew, we'd gotten our shots and we were finally finished after a marathon five days of chasing the Pope. Elated and exhausted, I saw a friendly looking woman from the Fox affiliate in DC and I asked her to take a picture of me and my crew, capturing the moment we could all begin to enjoy a well-earned rest. She asked us to take a half step to my left into a small vacant space on the tarmac. I looked down to the ground and saw the empty space was taped off.

Then I read the three capital letters written in yellow paint inside the empty box: CBS.

Sorry guys.

***

In Berlin I look down at my hands. The same hands that held the ashtray were the same hands that jumped on a camera and sent shots of the Pope to viewers around the world. I have a very tiny scar on my right hand at the base of my thumb. It is Y shaped. It is the exact same scar my friend Larry has. A tiny red and white split, healed over after twenty years but not quite faded away. We obtained our scars in Monterey, California on a shoot, using a wheelchair to move the camera around. A wheelchair is known in the television business as a poor man's dolly, a smooth way to move the camera without professional gear. Bored while we waited for our interview subjects to show up, Larry and I set up an obstacle course and conducted wheelchair races. We took turns careening around the room to beat one another's time. Laughing uncontrollably, we both were slamming our right thumbs against the brake of the wheelchair until our hands bled. I couldn't have understood back then how this would bond Larry and me. The scar is just a gentle reminder of the fun experiences we've shared. I bet they are still trying to buff out the black marks we left all over that linoleum floor. Sometimes a little memory has a lot of meaning in the long run. Good friends are hard to find. So are matching scars.

***

June 12th through the 15th, 1997, I was working a gig with Larry for the Golf Channel at The Congressional Country Club in Bethesda, Md. There, a mere few feet away from me, were the greatest names in the sport: Jack, Fuzzy, Tiger. No, it's not a Winnie the Pooh story. It was the US Open – for everyone but the golfers, a week of fun, parties and drunken revelry. As a freelance camera operator for a major sports network I had full access. The tournament was exciting and marked Tiger Woods' first US Open as a pro. By Sunday, the final day of the four-day event, there was a four-way tie as the leaders approached the back nine. I was in the press tent waiting for the post-tournament press conference. The tension in the press tent was high. Everyone was riveted to NBC's coverage on TV.

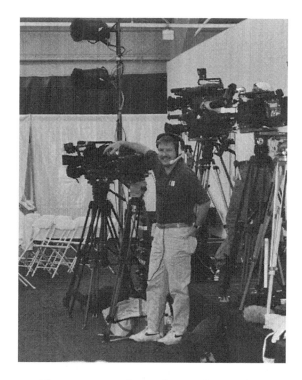

In the swamp with cameramen from all over the world at The US Open.

Suddenly, an explosion of cheers went up when South African Ernie Els took the lead. I thought maybe he was a nice guy and a favorite of the jaded press that followed the game around. But Ernie Els, nicknamed The Big Easy for his cool fluid swing, wasn't particularly liked. The media people in the press tent cheered because *anyone* had taken the lead. Before this surge, the tournament was tied and a tie meant a playoff and a playoff meant hanging around the golf course for an extra day. Absolutely *no one* in the press wanted to work an extra day. For example, one camera operator from New Zealand leaned over and confided in me,

"Tomorrow is my day off and I want to see some sights before I go home. The last place I want to be is dragging around this golf course, mate."

It was a balmy, mid-June afternoon and by dusk Ernie Els had held on to win. A wave of joy ran through the press tent to the sound of beer bottles popping open as no one in the room faced the dire prospect of having to work the next day.

Soon Els, Tiger Woods and a few others were in the press tent with us and the energy in the room surged again. I shot the press conference and then the area began to clear as people started coiling cables and packing up their bags. Smiles were everywhere. As coolers of beer started to empty, reporters exchanged souvenirs and things began to get loose.

By 9:45 PM most of the press had left to carry on the party elsewhere but my crew had to stay. I moved my camera and some lights from the press tent out to a makeshift set near the putting green in front of the clubhouse.

We were scheduled to shoot a live interview around 10:00 PM and the guest was Ernie Els' trainer. When he showed up, he'd brought the champion's golf bag with him as a prop. I wanted to put it between the two stools on the set, but it sat too low, so I dragged out a camera case to put under it and, as I hoisted it up, I said to the producer,

"Am I holding the winner's bag?"

"Yes, you are," he beamed.

Realizing that a professional golfer's clubs are the tools of his trade I reverently set the bag on the camera case and returned behind my camera. The trainer and the interviewer took their seats and almost instantly we were live on the air... for about ten seconds, that is. Then the word came we were losing the satellite. You must rent the time and our time was up. The producer ran up to me and screamed, "Give me your headset!"

He put it on and shouted at the director back in the studio, "This interview is gold! Get me more time!"

Quickly we received the green light for more satellite time and we were back on the air. While I shot the interview going out on live television, a bunch of South African friends of Ernie Els came stumbling out of the clubhouse and over toward us. They had been celebrating for a few hours by then and the producer welcomed them over but whispered for them to be quiet. Then the producer pulled out his personal cooler and distributed beer to everyone.

As the interview continued, the group was trying desperately to be quiet, but like schoolchildren they couldn't contain themselves and started giggling. The muted laughter became contagious and the producer was caught up in it, too.

One of the guys broke into a handstand and I could slowly feel the party turning full-tilt, right next to the live interview, just out of my shot. The trainer and the interviewer could feel it too but the viewing audience at home and the director back at the studio had no idea this was going on just off camera. They could only see the two people on the stools.

Then the party group just off camera noticed a huge US Open banner attached to a twenty-foot flagpole right next to me. I heard them whispering, deciding it would make a perfect souvenir. One guy shimmied up the flagpole and tried to pull it down, but he couldn't reach the little arm holding it on. Everyone in this group was now holding their hands to their faces, trying not to laugh out loud as the guy desperately reached for the banner.

A few feet away we were still going out live on the air with the interview. Frustrated, the pole climber slid back down the flagpole without his prize.

What happened next caught everyone by surprise. The flagpole guy bolted into my shot, smiled, and slipped the nine iron out of the champion's bag. The formerly-muted crowd now let out a loud cheer. I looked over at the producer to see his reaction, but he was on the ground, doubled over with laughter. In my headset, I heard the director back at the studio say, "What the hell is that? What the hell is that?"

The flagpole guy held up the club, curtsied, and exited from the camera's view. I heard the director say, "What the fuck is going on up there, Dugan?"

Like the viewers at home, he could only see the two guys on the stools. Meanwhile, the flagpole guy shimmied back up the pole, clutching the nine iron. He took a swipe at the banner but couldn't get it to fall.

He began to climb higher and higher, with the crowd cheering him on, but as he climbed, the aluminum pole began to sway. The interview somehow continued but I was convinced that the flagpole was going to buckle and fall right on Ernie Els' trainer with a 200-pound drunk South African guy crushing our interview subject to death live on national television.

Amused at the prospect and knowing full-well I wasn't in charge, I started laughing, too. I glanced back at the guy who *was* in charge, the producer. He was toasting the flagpole guy and seemed to be reveling in the chaos.

The flagpole guy was high up now and began to clank at the top of the pole with the nine iron. In my headset, I heard the director say, "What's that sound, Dugan?"

Suddenly, the pole took a big sway and everyone gasped. The flagpole guy screamed and the entire bunch howled with laughter, but the pole didn't fall. In my headset I heard, "Dugan! Dugan! What the hell is going on up there?"

Thankfully things calmed down for a moment as the frazzled flagpole guy slid down safely, but without the banner. He walked over to the cooler, opened another beer and stared at the flagpole. It seemed as if the interview might continue without any more disruptions. Then the flagpole guy had a revelation. Could the pole be pulled out of the ground? I heard a brief discussion then a couple of the guys got on it and *POP!* out it came. I looked up to see it sway precariously over my head for a moment then it crashed to the ground with a mighty thud, *WHOMP!* right on the putting green, inches away from the trainer. Once again, in my headset I heard, "Good God, Dugan! What the hell was that?"

Oblivious to the live interview, the party guys ran into my shot, pulled off their souvenir banner and started to dance around with it. I heard the director say, "Dugan! Talk to me! What the fuck is going on?"

I didn't know what to say so I just kept shooting. The brave interviewer remained professional and plowed forward with his interview of the trainer, live on the air but the producer now could barely contain himself as he and the others howled with laughter. The party group all exchanged high fives and the sound of beer cans opening were now being picked up on the microphones. I heard the Director say, "I think you guys are having a party up there, Dugan."

Then I heard the producer whisper to the flagpole guy, "Tell you what - when I give you the signal, walk past the camera on your hands!"

Caught up in the fun I zoomed out to a wide shot. Egged on by his friends, the flagpole guy began to walk across the putting green right into my shot upside-down, on his hands. The interview stopped as the upended flagpole guy's shirt fell and his full belly hung out, live, on national television. He got to the center of the green and collapsed in laughter. Undaunted, he bounced back up off the grass and stumbled off.

In my headset, I heard the Director scream, "What the hell was that! Who's that guy, Dugan? What the hell is going on up there?!"

The trainer and the interviewer fell apart laughing and a very loud off-camera belch was heard. The Director said, "Damn it, that's it! Screw it. Fade to black! Cut back to the studio!"

Mercifully, our live US Open coverage came to an end. At that we just laughed, dimmed the lights, and opened the remaining beers.

We all drank as Ernie Els' trainer distributed souvenir golf balls to everyone from the champion's bag.

5

As I ponder the memories and the people I've encountered I realize that it is almost as difficult to know yourself as it is to know others. Examining my life, putting it all here on paper, it's not easy to decide what to put in and what to leave out. I left out the stories of acting beside Al Pacino, telling jokes in a movie theater with Barry Levinson and discovering decades later that I was in the same scene in a John Waters film as my dentist.

But it is easy to recall what my big break was. For years I tried to get into the Discovery Channel. I looked at the network like a box. Most people try to get into a box from the opening on the top and when they can't they give up. I looked at the sides, the bottom, the corners. I held the box up to the light. I was determined to get inside.

I tried sending resumes and filling out applications but nothing traditional seemed to be working. Then a friend of mine attended a class where Mark Kozaki from Discovery came in to speak. Kozaki told the class that they could contact him if they had any questions. I wasn't in the class but I called Kozaki anyway.

He was very kind and I called him twice a year for a few years. After completing a small documentary, I invited Kozaki and some of his Discovery friends to a premiere. I rented a hall and asked my friends to bring food, telling the Discovery folks that the event was catered. Kozaki just happened to bring Dave Shapiro who was looking to expand Discovery's pool of freelance editors.

The day after the premiere Shapiro called me and I got my big break. I began to freelance at Discovery using vacation time from my other job. When I felt I'd made a good enough impression I left that job to become a fulltime freelancer again, even though by this time I had a wife and family. But the folks I worked with at Discovery encouraged me and I made the leap of faith. Then, after a few months, Discovery offered me a staff position.

I was in.

The network had launched in 1985 and by the time I came onboard ten years later they were still relatively small. Most of the network revolved around the seventh floor of a nondescript office building in Bethesda, Maryland on the outskirts of Washington, DC. Working for The Discovery Channel in the early days was like riding a rocket ship that just kept climbing higher and higher. (When it came time for me to publish this book I called my publishing company Rocket Ship Press as a tribute to those early years.)

When I first arrived, the company was like a family. The people working there were happy, dedicated, and the company was continuing to grow. Cable TV was still finding its way and people all around me were literally creating the future of home entertainment, experimenting, and willing to try anything that made sense.

All kinds of things were tried out. Someone thought a live show would be cool, but, if I remember correctly, the first experiment at Discovery with live TV didn't go so well.

The idea was to set up a camera at a pond in Africa and watch the various animals as they came up to drink. This prime-time event went off without a hitch - except no one remembered to tell the animals. It was an hour consisting of two British guys whispering off camera about what might happen. I don't think a single animal showed up except for a small bird, something you could watch out your own window at home. But the experimentation and growth continued and, as the company grew, I grew with it.

When I arrived, Discovery had already purchased and re-launched TLC. Soon I was witnessing the birth of Animal Planet, the Science Channel and a myriad of other new domestic networks. My department serviced them all.

I started out doing cut-to-clocks. A cut-to-clock involves taking an hour long show and cutting it down to create time for commercials, then figuring out where those commercials should fall.

A finished, hour-long documentary program would be delivered with a running time somewhere between fifty-two and fifty-eight minutes. It was my job to watch it, cut it down to forty-four minutes without the viewer knowing anything was omitted, then drop in four commercial breaks at times that seemed to make sense. I was given a broadcast 'clock' to follow, which looked like a pie chart representing an hour of programming time.

Each network had a slightly different clock but the principles were the same. The first and third breaks had to land somewhere within a predetermined window. For example, the first break had to fall between three minutes and eighteen minutes after the top of the hour. These were called local avails. That's when a portion of the commercial break became available to the local cable affiliate.

If you watch a network carefully you can pretty much tell which commercials are local and which ones are from the network but it's not always easy as national companies often buy commercial time – or "spots" - on local stations. The other two commercial breaks without local avails were for the network to sell their own commercials as well as time to promote other network shows.

I became proficient at this style of editing. I'd watch the show as I digitized it into the editing system, making notes about what I wanted to take out and where a good break might fall. I tried to make the first break occur as late as possible, usually around quarter past the hour, figuring that would set the hook for the viewer, getting them involved in the story for fifteen uninterrupted minutes and making them less likely to change the channel.

I also tried to make the fourth and final commercial break close to but not at the end of the show, giving the viewer a little something to hold on for. That left trying to find a good spot for the other two breaks.

After a while I was adept at this and I could bang out a cut-to-clock show in under two hours: an hour to watch and upload it and an hour to make the edits. My bosses liked my efficiency and praised my work. Soon I was training other editors on cut-to-clocks.

In those days, virtually all the brass at the networks worked on the same floor as me and I could just pop my head into anyone's door for a chat. After cutting down a show called *The Ten Deadliest Snakes in the World* hosted by Croc Hunter Steve Irwin, I struck up a conversation with the Executive Producer. She relayed a funny story about the shoot that went something like this.

"Irwin is notoriously fearless. But his camera operator is not. The problem is his crew must go everywhere Steve goes. On *Deadliest Snakes* Irwin went deep into some remote murky swamp to find examples. Remember, these are among the deadliest snakes in the world and the swamp is full of them. At one point Irwin jumps out of the boat and into waist-deep blackish water and heads off. Well, the camera operator has to follow him. Now they're both far into the swamp, waist-deep in this black water and Irwin says, 'These waters are full of deadly snakes. Ooh, they're hitting my legs. There must be hundreds of them.' Can you imagine being the camera operator on that shoot?

"The third deadliest snake is found in cane fields because the fields are full of rats that come to eat the cane and the snakes feed on the rats. So, they go into this cane which is creepy because you can't see anything around you. They don't find anything because its summer in Australia and hot and the snakes and rats are all underground. The camera operator thinks he's going to get off easy until Irwin says, 'Let's come back at night.' Now they go back and its pitch dark except for the little lights they bring. If the cane fields were creepy during the day, they're petrifying at night. And the place is absolutely crawling with rats feasting on the cane. Then Irwin finds a snake. Its gigantic, like over six feet long. And its pissed off. Now tell me Jeff, who can you get to be camera operator on a shoot like that?

"Next they take a light plane to an island whose name translates to *The Island That Moves*, because it is literally covered with snakes. After they land, the population of the island goes up to three - Irwin, the camera operator and the pilot. The pilot says, 'I'm going to take off and circle while you shoot. I don't want a plane full of snakes.' So, the pilot takes off leaving Irwin and the camera operator alone on this God-forsaken island. It doesn't take long for the snakes to come out and check out the new arrivals. At one point the camera operator says, 'Uhm, Steve. I think one of those poisonous snakes just crawled up inside my pants leg.' Irwin replies, 'Don't worry. He'll leave if he doesn't see anything he likes.' No one ever thinks of the poor camera operator who has to chase this guy all over the planet."

Unfortunately, in 2006 Steve Irwin died far too young, not at the jaws of a crocodile or a deadly snake, but in a freak accident while swimming above a stingray whose tail spike struck Irwin in the heart.

Of the hundreds of programs, I cut down only once did any of our networks hear a complaint. It was a one-up for TLC. A 'one-up' is a stand-alone documentary, not part of a series. I forget what the show was about but it ended with a mock emergency that was full of bad acting and I felt it was superfluous to the show. It was an easy omission. After it aired the producers called the network and threatened to sue asking, "How could you cut out the dramatic conclusion?"

Mary Ellen Iwata was the TLC executive that took the call. I knew Mary Ellen from my *Evening Magazine* days as she was the Executive Producer there for a while but that wasn't going to get me a free pass. Mary Ellen was tough and had fought her way to the top with a clever wit and a boatload of tenacity. In short, she didn't take crap from anybody. I was called into her office to explain.

She backed me up and from then on suggested producers deliver the programs already cut to clock so they can omit what they wanted to. I liked that idea because it freed up me and my department to do even more interesting work. And we did.

John Ford was the top dog at TLC in those days and he nicknamed us 'The Department of Alchemy." We got into all kinds of things.

It's amazing that, in those days, decisions I made went right on the air without anyone scrutinizing me. The shows made sense, the viewers never knew the content they were missing and I was soon rewarded with additional responsibilities.

Soon I moved into creating bumps. Bumps are the short elements that appear as the show goes to commercial break, for example: "Coming up: The Croc Hunter takes on his most dangerous assignment yet – after the break." If the bump occurred as the program was going to commercial that was called a 'bump out.' As the show returned after the commercial, a 'bump in' example was, "You're watching the Croc Hunter on Animal Planet. Now back to the show…"

Once I began to write copy, I also got to produce the bump narrations - a fun, new responsibility.

Each network within the Discovery family of networks had chosen a specific voice talent and the staff producers would be told when he or she was in the studio. I might be told that I have time with the talent on Tuesday from 1:00 to 1:30 PM, then possibly again on Friday morning.

For Discovery, the voice was Bill St. James. Bill would go to a sound studio in New York and I'd fax the copy, call up the studio and produce the bumps over the phone. I had to use my time wisely and get the most out of the talent while I had him. Usually bump outs were unique for each break but bump ins were generic. For example, if the bump in simply said something like, "Now back to the show" I could use it after all four of the breaks and I'd only get Bill to say it once. This saved time since Bill was in demand in those days and my time with him was valuable.

Fortunately, Bill was charming and easy to work with. He was a fun guy with a wicked sense of humor and he loved it when we tried to slip in something rude just to trip him up - which we often did - much in the way I observed during that early Flite Three session with Forrest Tucker. Some of the most outlandish voiceovers were edited into little shows that were circulated around the office but never made it out of the building.

If we had some extra time with the talent we often had fun recording special birthday greetings to friends with these great voices. Many producers had a voice talent record the out-going message for their telephone answering machines, for both home and work.

Like many places in the television business, the unofficial clothes color at Discovery was black – and *no one wore a tie*. The saying is 'If a producer shows up wearing a tie, let him do your taxes but don't let him produce your show.'

Bob Sitrick was hired to develop innovative engineering ideas for the network and he relocated from Comedy Central in New York. Dressing to impress during his first few days at Discovery he wore a tie. By Friday I saw him in the hall and said, "Dude, enough with the tie already – *you got the gig!*" A great guy, Bob just laughed - but he never wore a tie to the office again.

By the mid 90's, cable stations were expanding so fast it was hard for viewers to tell one network from the other. Around this time networks decided to put their logos in the lower right corner of the screen. These small, half-transparent logos are called 'bugs.'

One afternoon Sitrick called me from the uplink facility, a remote building where the signals are sent up to a satellite for distribution all over the world. Sitrick informed me that it was time to try out Discovery's very first bug, a spinning globe with the word "Discovery" written under it. He asked me to turn on my TV and tell him how it looked. I did. Soon the logo popped onto the screen. Over the phone I told Sitrick, "a litter darker … no… too much … a little lighter … yeah, raise it up… that looks good."

Anyone else who happened to be watching that afternoon saw our adjustments live on the air as they happened.

Sitrick quickly became the guy who had to figure out how to pull off all the big ideas people were coming up with and he was great at it.

For example, the idea of live broadcasts were still tempting and when Discovery decided to go live from the wreckage of the Titanic in 1998 it was left to Sitrick to try and figure out how. Over a year of planning led to this historic expedition and Sitrick pioneered new technology to pull it off. He helped to link up manned and unmanned submersibles two-and-a-half miles under the ocean to create the first ever live broadcast of its kind.

In addition to technical planning and overseeing the operations of the broadcast, Sitrick dove with the team that photographed a twenty-ton piece of the Titanic hull as it approached the surface tethered to lift bags. This "Watch with The World" event was broadcast live on Discovery networks around the world simultaneously. I was impressed.

Other challenges for Bob included going live from remote Bikini Atoll during Shark Week. Whatever they threw at him, Sitrick rose to the occasion.

One day I was sitting in his office with him watching a live press conference when John Hendricks, the founder of Discovery, announcing to the world that the network was going to launch the country's first high definition television network. Sitrick turned to me and said, "What the hell did he say that for? How are we going to do *that?*"

I replied, "Well, I guess it's up to you to figure it out, Bob."

Of course, he did.

Bob Sitrick and I race jet skis on the boardwalk in Ocean City, Maryland at a
Discovery Team Build while Dave Shapiro looks on.
Photo courtesy of Jo Ann Burton.

Meanwhile, I was given a reversion to produce. A 'reversion' is a new
version of an existing show. The network would often purchase the
rights to a series from England or Germany or France and the script
would need to be rewritten and a new narration produced with an
American narrator.

I'd also need to create a new title sequence, maybe buy or shoot some
new footage and create a new sound mix.

I'd look at the show, rewrite the script, often taking out British terms
like "duvet" and "jumper" and replace them with "blanket" and
"sweater." The result would be a show that sounded like a US
product, only all the interviews were with people from another
country.

It's amazing how forgiving the viewing public is when it comes to reversions. If I did my job well most viewers simply couldn't tell it was a reworked program. The process was fun because I could inject even more creative writing into my work, dream up some interesting titles and select the new narrator myself.

The first time I was asked to create a budget for a reversion I carefully plotted out the needs, tried to forecast all that was necessary, padded a small percent for possible overages and submitted it to my boss, the wonderful Susie Miles.

"I think it'll cost ten thousand dollars," I said.

She didn't look up but continued to type away at her computer, then paused, tilted her head slightly and said, "Take twenty. You never know…"

Coming from my previous job where we had to make magic with no budget whatsoever I walked away thinking, "I'm going to enjoy this."

Boy, was I right.

To cast a narrator for a show, I'd work with agents in Washington and New York since that was where the east coast talent congregated. It would start with me faxing an agent a paragraph of my script. The next day I'd receive a CD with over twenty professional narrators reading what I'd written. I'd make my selection, fax the agent my entire script and set up a recording session.

I felt that I could confidently produce short-form pieces like bumps over the phone but never trusted that scheme to produce a narration for an hour-long documentary. In fact, I only did that once and regretted it.

I flew to Los Angeles to work with Peri Gilpin, best known as Roz on Frasier, for a one-up on TLC. The only problem was Gilpin fell ill and couldn't do the session. Rather than fly home and back again I opted to fly home and produce the show over the phone. When it came back there were four subtle little nuances I would've changed had I been there in the studio.

Today, there is so much poorly produced content online that the standards for quality seem to have significantly diminished. But I still like to get it right.

The company had no problem sending me wherever I felt I needed to go to get the job done. Either I had to go to the talent or the talent had to come to me. Most often in those days I'd go to New York to produce a session. I've always loved the city and it was only a few hours away by train. And Discovery would pick up the tab, sending me first class.

I'd usually train up in the morning and head straight for the studio. I could work anywhere I wanted and I'd often choose a recording studio in midtown like Buttons Sounds, a little boutique place run by Rich Macar. Rich's wife was an amazing interior designer and the comfortably furnished studio was like a welcoming little oasis in bustling Manhattan.

Sessions for a one-hour documentary might take around three or four hours, and one of the perks of the job was booking enough time to enjoy a great lunch. The studios would provide me with a thick book full of menus from local restaurants. We'd generally work for a couple of hours, take a break, select from the lunch book and someone would deliver the lunch to the studio. Lunch with the narrator was always a good time to share stories, check up on industry gossip and learn about one another.

And when the session was over, there was usually enough time for a little shopping in Manhattan, a nice dinner with friends, an overnight stay in a great hotel and then a leisurely train ride back the next morning. Too often networks and independent producers try and squeeze every penny out of their people working crews up to sixteen hours a day.

But this was television production the way it should be.

Civilized.

There were other perks to being part of a thriving, emerging television network. Because we worked together so often I became friends with some of the top talent agents in New York. My favorite was Lisa Marber Rich, who runs Atlas Talent. If I needed something in the city – from a weird prop to a ticket to the hottest show - Lisa always knew how to get it. And when I needed talent, Lisa could deliver.

One night after a recording session we went to a comedy club she'd been asked to visit. Several comedians were vying to get her to represent them and she wanted my opinion of them. Later, at the bar, she introduced me to a few members of the Muppets, whom she also represented. The show was great, we had a blast and I never laughed so hard. I don't know if she signed anybody that night but I know it was just plain fun to hang out for a while and get a glimpse into the world of one of the top talent agents in Manhattan. I'm happy to say we remain friends.

When you work for a network - and have the money to do things right - people want to work with you. During one trip to New York in November of 1997, a new production house wanted me to swing by for a visit. To try to lure my business, the rep offered me four tickets to a taping of the Oprah Winfrey Show. By this time the same Oprah that had come to Flite Three to cut promos had become a star. She had the hottest daytime program and drew the biggest names in the business. "Who's the guest?" I asked.

"Paul McCartney," came the reply.

That was an easy decision. I loved the Beatles and the chance to be in the same room with Paul was thrilling – plus the guy from the studio also said I could bring up to three friends.

I invited Lisa, another Discovery producer who was a big Beatles fan and her best friend. When I recall this story at parties, I always hear, "Why didn't you invite me?"

When the big day arrived the four of us met in midtown and walked to the venue. At the intersection across from where the taping would take place we stopped and waited for the traffic light to change. While we stood there on the corner, a long black limousine pulled up right next to us, waiting for the light. I said to my friends, "I bet Paul McCartney is in that limo."

Just then the darkened rear window lowered and *there he was!*

All I could muster was, "Hi Paulie!"

We were only a few feet away. We all stood there with our mouths gaping as he raised a yellow disposable camera and snapped our photograph. With that we took one step toward the limo but Paul raised a finger, stopping us in our tracks.

The darkened window rose back up, the traffic light changed and the limo pulled away. We couldn't believe our luck and shared a manic group hug on the corner. Later, during the *Oprah* taping, Paul explained that he was taking photos of his trip for his wife Linda, who was back home ill. Less than five months later, Paul's beloved wife of nearly three decades passed away from cancer.

Somewhere, in a shoebox on Paul McCartney's farm in Scotland, is a photograph of me standing on the corner in Manhattan with three friends and a shocked look on my face.

What a great time it was to be working for The Discovery Channel and its family of networks. It truly felt like The Land of Opportunity in those heady days and the work really flowed.

I wrote and produced countless narrations. Shows with crazy titles like *Baboons: Too Close for Comfort, Crater of Death* and *When Pigs Ruled the World.* I could literally write something, record it with a narrator and then watch it on TV along with millions of people around the world. I reversioned hundreds of shows, learning about thought-provoking subjects with documentaries like *The Sleep Files, Lions of the Kalahari, The Search for Sunken Treasure* and *The Spanish-American War.*

One TLC show I worked on, called *Alien Autopsy,* didn't require me to do much on it but when the credits appeared at the end I guess my name popped out somehow because I got more calls from friends who saw that show than just about anything I had ever worked on.

In those days, when shows were delivered they had to come from the producers with certain elements attached. We'd get the audio in 'mix minus narration.' That meant the original audio mix with the original foreign narrator was on the tape in stereo on tracks one and two, and the audio mix *minus the narration* was in stereo on tracks three and four. That way I could use the mix minus narration tracks to create a new version with a new narrator.

If we were lucky we'd get all the original tracks 'split out.' That meant I had all the tracks isolated, up to 24, so I could remix every sound effect, all the music, the natural sound, the interviews and create an entirely new mix. This was a much better way to work since I could 'sweeten' the mix, adding new sounds to complement the picture, replace the music if I wanted to and make the audio experience much more vibrant and robust.

One reversion, a Discovery Pictures Production called *Polar Bears: Survival on the Ice* was delivered with all the elements split out. My audio engineer for that project was a dirt bike racer named Frank Ayd and the son of the guy who gave me my first break at Flite Three.

We spent days sweetening up this program that tracked the life of a polar bear family. We wanted every crunching step on the snow, each nuzzle between the mother and her cubs, every blast of arctic wind to be heard. The result was a show that really transported the viewer into the world of these polar bears and it netted us some international recognition for the mix – a Wildscreen Panda Award, known as the Oscars of the natural history and wildlife film industry.

Working at Discovery was like a paid education, complete with the chance to have fun and be creative.

Once I was given a particularly challenging series to work on from the Travel Channel. I loved working for the Travel Channel and after Discovery purchased the network and re-launched it I knew it was the place for me.

The network bought a half-dozen programs from a French distributor that were beautifully photographed but had virtually no script. There were long, unbroken shots where there was no narration, followed by an obscure French poem. It was hard to tell what was going on and far from compelling television. But the images were spectacular.

I watched those shows over and over with the sound down and began to craft a story for each of them. This technique is called 'writing to picture' - and it isn't as easy as it sounds. You can't just tell the viewer what they're seeing – you must tell them what they're *not* seeing.

One of the episodes was about winter crab fishing in Alaska. I researched the location and wrote about the temperature of the water and how quickly a person would die of exposure if they fell into the ocean. I wrote about the struggle to survive under extreme conditions and what it must feel like at the end of a long, cold, sunless day. I decided to call the show, *The Most Dangerous Place to Live in the U.S.* When it aired it was a smash hit, helping the Travel Channel hit their best ratings week to date.

Years later, I learned from my friend Lori Rothschild how my reversion helped inspire another Discovery program. Lori wrote to me, "I still think of you every time I think of *Deadliest Catch*... I can tell you that I showed your little show to Jane Root and Abby Greensfelder. They screened it and sent Original Productions off to do a taster. The taster came back, cut to Bon Jovi's *Dead or Alive.* I remember screening it with the team and we all had shivers... we knew we had a hit."

The Emmy-award-winning *Deadliest Catch* went on to become one of Discovery Channel's most popular and longest-running series. It's fun to know I had a small hand in helping to inspire something so successful.

Other titles I reversioned in that French series for the Travel Channel included *The World's Most Dangerous Port* and *Last of the Lone Cowboys.* *Port* did great ratings that year, even up against the Olympics, but I loved the little show called *Last of the Lone Cowboys.*

By the time I sat down to write that I'd really begun to have fun with these scripts and I wrote a lot of myself into that show. The program had long portions where the cowboy just looked off into the distance, and I wrote about what it must feel like to be alone for six months at a time and how the craziness of modern life contrasts that of a cowboy. As I wrote, I knew people all over the world in all kinds of places and circumstances would hear my own little philosophies about slowing down and appreciating the world around you. What a great feeling.

My biggest success with the French series came from a show I called *Best Place to Brave the Wild Sea.* It was about little islands off the coast of France where the lighthouses are battered by incredible waves. I wrote about the people and their courage and the drive they had inside of them. There were a lot of character voices to re-create and the sound mix was tricky but when it was over I knew I had taken a show with no story and crafted a documentary that was something special.

When it aired, *Best Place to Brave the Wild Sea* set a new Nielsen ratings record for the Travel Channel, a record that would take another three years to break.

I loved going to work since, in those days, work was always something different. I wound up having to become a minor subject matter expert on a wide variety of interesting topics. It was very intellectually stimulating. I also met a variety of very interesting people.

One day TLC acquired a program on aviation disasters but it needed a lot of work. I researched the disasters, bought some additional footage, wrote a new script and called the show simply, *Air Disasters.* I did a talent search and selected a guy from New York I'd never worked with before. He had a great voice and, as it turned out, a funny story.

I was working at a new audio facility in Northern Virginia and arranged to fly him down, have him picked up at the airport in a private car and brought to the studio. The session went well and soon it was time for lunch. Our food order was brought in and set down before us and I immediately saw this guy's face turn ashen as he wistfully stared down at the box on the table. I could tell something had profoundly affected him and asked, "Is everything OK?"

He took a deep sigh and said, "Let me tell you a story… About ten years ago, my wife and I were invited to an investor's party in Greenwich Village. We weren't interested in investing but the two guys throwing the party were nice people and we decided to go.

"They were a couple of lawyers who wanted to open a new restaurant and they were looking for partners. We showed up at their apartment with about a half dozen other people and we all sat at the kitchen table while the two guys cooked.

"They had an idea the public needed some new and different kind of pizzas. They cooked and we ate. It was good.

"So then came the pitch. My wife and I knew most new restaurants fail in the first year so, even before we showed up, we told each other that we would *not* invest. Everybody else liked what they ate and decided to put up ten thousand dollars.

"So, these two guys opened their restaurant. You know what they called it? California Pizza Kitchen. Last year everyone but my wife and I who were sitting at that kitchen table got a million-dollar bonus check for Christmas."

He paused and stared out the window. I looked down at the box on the table. It read California Pizza Kitchen, a restaurant chain in ten countries with over a half-billion dollars in annual revenue.

According to the founder's website 22 of the 23 people they asked to invest said yes. And I was sitting across the table from the one guy who didn't. I could literally feel his heart sink.

Trying to lighten the mood, I told him about the time my ex-father-in-law told me about a new company coming to Maryland, asking me if I thought it would be a good investment.

"It's called "Jiffy Lube," he'd said.

I told him, "No way - I change my own oil."

Now the largest company of its kind, Jiffy Lube changes my oil, too. Yet another example of my inability to see into the future. I guessed neither this narrator nor I would ever make a fortune as investors.

Air Disasters went on to become a big hit for TLC.

Soon I was assigned to re-narrate another four-part series on aviation disasters that TLC had acquired from the UK. It was called *Survival in the Sky*. I screened it and the visuals were well-crafted but the script needed some work. I spent days reworking the scripts and selected Will Lyman as the voice talent.

Will, the voice of *Frontline* on PBS and the national voice of BMW in America and the guy who voices 'the most interesting man in the world' commercials was, and is still, one of the best voices anywhere on earth. We'd worked together on many successful programs and I felt he had the right tone to take this important series to the next level.

I designed a new title sequence and flew to Boston to cut the narration with Will. In the studio Will was a wonder. Most narrators need at least a little guidance, especially on pace. I would often ask a narrator to slow down in a session, letting the words carry more weight, letting them resonate for the viewer. Will was so professional he practically produced himself. And his tone is haunting – he really knows how to draw you into a story.

There is an old saying that goes 'don't use a battle ax when you can do the same job with a razor blade.' Will knows what that means when it comes the art of narration. He is a master of his craft.

I felt this series was strong to begin with but with a beefed-up script and Will's golden tones, I knew we were really onto something.

I went to see Steve Cheskin, the Chief of Production for TLC at the time, and told him I thought we really had something here. Remember, in those days, I could walk down the hall and poke my head into the door of practically anyone at any of Discovery's networks. I asked Steve to throw a little promotion money at it and it might really pop in the ratings. Steve trusted me and went along with my instincts.

When *Survival in the Sky* aired, the series earned TLC its highest Nielsen primetime ratings ever recorded up until that time.

And I had delivered another hit.

As a result, TLC asked me to do another program on air disasters – and then another. Finally, after doing four series on air disasters I asked my boss to please give the next one to another producer because I already knew too much about air disasters and if I had any more exposure to this material I'd never fly again!

Fortunately for me the one statistic I focused on came at the end of episode one of *Survival in the Sky*: "One comforting thought… if you boarded a jet at random every single day, it would be 26,000 years on average before you were involved in a major crash. And even then, the odds are you'd survive."

In July 1998, the Travel Channel bought the North American rights to a French travel series featuring a guy named Antoine and the network asked me to reversion it. Almost no one in the United States had ever heard of Antoine but he was a *huge* star in France. I screened a few episodes and really liked it.

Antoine was a wild-haired freak - an old French hippie - and very charming on screen. I took on the project and got to work.

Since the series was originally in French, the Paris production company that sold it to us contractually agreed to provide a clean copy with mix-minus narration. 'Clean' means a copy of the final edited show with no subtitles, opening titles or any writing on the screen so we could add our own. Well, the French production company failed to deliver a clean version.

I phoned the production company in Paris. Due to the time difference, there was only a few-hour window to call Paris from the east coast of the U.S. and they couldn't find the producer so I'd have to leave a message and wait a second day. The next day, when I finally reached someone who would listen to me they stalled and stammered. They would not promise me a clean version.

I threatened the production company with breach of contract and said I might just hop on a plane and come get the tapes myself. But they still wouldn't commit to sending anything. By this time, it was late July and I knew that if I didn't get the clean copy by the end of the month, I'd lose another month as virtually everyone who lives and works in Paris leaves for the month of August. I was desperate. So, the next day I called my Parisian Fixer.

Every producer needs a 'fixer' sometimes. A producer has a lot of people looking for guidance during a production – editors, writers, graphic artists, audio guys, network executives – and to keep pushing a production forward sometimes you need a little help. A fixer is just that – someone who fixes things. You give the fixer the problem, whatever it is, *and he'll fix it.*

For example, did the caterer deliver the wrong meal to a temperamental actor? Fix it. Did the crew get shut out of their hotel and a convention has all the hotels in town booked? Call the fixer. You get the idea.

In a complicated production where time is money and there is a lot going on, the producer does not always have time to stop and deal with these types of problems; hence, the role of the fixer was born.

By this time my old friend Dzl from Flite Three had moved to Paris. Unable to find much work, Dzl had made a brilliant transition. He had tried to find work as an audio engineer but when French producers heard his command of English, he became an English voice talent. Now visitors to Monte Carlo would turn on the TV in their hotel rooms and hear Dzl describe things like the features of the hotel. He quickly learned he could make a lot more money in a few hours as a voice talent than he could in a week scraping by as an audio engineer – and spend the rest of his time drinking coffee by the Seine.

By the time I asked him to be my fixer Dzl had lived in Paris for a few years. He knew his way around and had a good command of the language. He also understood the language of television production and knew what a clean copy was. In effect, Dzl was a perfect fit to become my Parisian Fixer.

I called Dzl and explained my dilemma. He knew right where the production company was located. He dropped everything, hopped on the Metro and then, in perfect French, burst in to their office and pretended to be me.

He started by flailing his arms in a fit, inventing a story about how I jumped on a plane in a rage and demanded the clean tapes or the entire contract would be torn to shreds. Dzl told me their eyes literally popped out of their heads. The production company was so impressed they dropped everything and made a clean copy of the series while he waited.

Dzl collected the tapes and marched right to the nearest Federal Express office. I had them the next day. My man! I love fixers. I wish they were available in all walks of life.

After watching the series over and over, I finally spoke to the original French host Antoine on the phone. His English wasn't bad. I felt he had such a strong personality on the show and such a feel for the material that it just made sense to have Antoine re-narrate the entire series in English.

I had his original French scripts quickly translated by my friend Laura Rodriguez's translation company and made arrangements for Antoine to come to the US for the recording sessions.

Just getting a message to Antoine was a challenge. He was often sailing on his 40-foot catamaran, *The Banana Split*. Unbelievably, Antoine had crossed the Atlantic and Pacific Oceans dozens of times alone in that little boat. He would sail for weeks all by himself, tying a rope to his leg when he felt like a swim.

These were the days before satellite phones and when Antoine wanted to communicate with someone – which wasn't often - he'd pull up next to a giant freighter at sea and ask the ship to send a fax. Can you picture that? Unbelievable.

When he approached a destination for a TV shoot – usually an exotic island somewhere – he would arrange to have a TV crew there waiting for him. This is how he made his French TV series. He seemed like a real adventurer. I loved the idea of working with him.

A little background: Antoine was a French pop star in late 1960's Paris. He had a monster hit called *Les Elucubrations* and rode it into a career. If you google that song, the music video is a hoot – and reminiscent of the times.

For the French, Antoine was epitome of the guy who never sold out, the old free spirit, and the French loved him. Every time he was in Paris, he'd appear as a guest on the hottest talk shows. His travel videos had set a French sales record for the fastest-selling home-video series. He had his own clothing line, his own cologne and was the major spokesperson for the biggest cell phone company in the country. In France, Antoine was a *brand*.

Meanwhile, summer was heating up for me.

Life at Discovery had become chaotic, full of travel commitments and conflicting obligations. August was a busy month as I flew to Los Angeles to produce a narration for a TLC show called *Sun Storms* with Jerry Doyle, an actor from a syndicated sci fi series called *Babylon 5*.

Then I spent some time with my family in Disneyland, flew back to New York to produce a Discovery show about marsupials, then it was on to Maine for a weekend with friends followed by a stop in Boston for a narration about lions, while mixing in a little freelancing and getting my son ready for his first day of kindergarten.

I was laying the groundwork for another big responsibility - a late-autumn trip to the Netherlands and France where I would garner my first credits as executive producer for a new TLC series called *Skybound*. Because of this pace, I had fallen out of the habit of paying attention to the news.

This would soon prove to be a costly error.

In Los Angeles producing the narration for Sun Storms with Jerry Doyle.

By the middle of September, I was ready to devote my time to Antoine and Antoine was ready to travel to America. Although I was looking forward to it I had a few reservations about working with him. Antoine was a big star in his home country and I had rewritten a lot of his original script to reflect the fact that he would not be easily recognized as a celebrity to an American audience.

Sensitive to cultural differences and language barriers, I wasn't confident I could convince Antoine that I was now the boss and we needed to change his script. His travel series was long, fourteen episodes, and I anticipated we'd encounter at least a few issues that needed to be diplomatically addressed.

I felt that perhaps my French celebrity needed some handling.

I concluded that the best way to deal with this situation would be with a neutral translator, someone who could eloquently state my case in perfect French to what might be a temperamental star.

Although I was keenly aware of the arrogant stereotype many Americans conjure up about the French I'd never experienced anything but nice, friendly people during my half-dozen trips to France but I was unsure what to think about Antoine.

He was already pouting about the fact TLC wouldn't fly him and his assistant, Francet, to the US in first class. I didn't want to get stuck, alone, with a prima donna and his entourage.

I did what any resourceful producer would do. I went back to my fixer.

I hired Dzl to fly over to act as my translator.

Discovery had just built a world-class production facility in Miami and that's where I chose to work. I also figured Antoine would enjoy the laid-back vibe of South Beach. On Sunday, September 20th, 1998, we rendezvoused in Miami and checked into a luxurious hotel right on the beach.

Since a narrator can't talk *all* day I structured our days like this - record in the morning, swim in the afternoon, wine and dine in the evening, then repeat. I unpacked and settled in for a week and a half of good work mixed with late summer sunshine and South Beach high jinx.

The way it should be.

Civilized.

Quickly we melded our cultures. Antoine turned me on to fine French Bordeaux wines (all blends it turns out) and I turned Antoine onto Taco Bell (never lose your taste for cheap food.) He loved it.

But something strange was going on around us. On our second

morning in Miami, while I sat on the balcony enjoying my first cup of coffee, I saw a large group of people hauling huge sheets of plywood.

That afternoon I glanced up from my beach towel and saw another group of people carrying huge jugs of water.

After dinner, I saw another group of folks wrestling with enormous sheets of plastic.

The next morning, I opened my hotel room door and looked down at the *Miami Herald* on my doorstep. There, by my foot, right on the front page, was a big color map with three arrows indicating the possible path of Hurricane Georges. The center arrow seemed to be pointing directly at my balcony.

A category-four hurricane was headed right for us and I didn't know it. It didn't take me long to realize I now had to tap that producer's best friend: Plan B.

I telephoned Discovery's Travel Department and asked them to please get us the hell out of there. They asked me where I wanted to go. I recalled a nice, boutique recording studio in Virginia that wanted my business. I made a hasty phone call, learned it was available and booked it for a week.

That evening we walked into a deserted Miami International Airport. It was a sight like none I'd ever seen. The entire terminal was empty. I mean empty. We breezed through security and walked down a long empty pier to a door where a dozen people stood in line. We boarded the plane and it pushed back, moving out to the runway, passing row after row of empty piers.

There were no other planes at the entire airport. Miami International is one of the busiest airports in the world with over eighty airlines serving around a hundred and fifty destinations and we were on the very last plane out. Thank you, Discovery Travel Department, – I still don't know how you did it. You guys are truly the best!

As we slipped silently into the night, I said a quiet prayer for those left behind.

Hurricane Georges eventually skirted Miami and slid along the Florida Keys before slamming into Biloxi, Mississippi. By the time it was over that hurricane had claimed over six hundred lives, causing eight billion dollars in damages.

Left, French singer-sailor Antoine holding a pumpkin, me on the right. Dzl, stands behind us sporting a Baltimore Orioles t-shirt.

Arriving safely in Virginia, we checked into a classic Colonial-style hotel owned by the evangelical preacher Pat Robertson. What a contrast to the hedonism of South Beach.

Across the street was a place called The Waffle House and it became our morning headquarters.

And so, a little routine began. Each morning, for the rest of the production, I'd meet Antoine in the lobby of the hotel where he'd say, "Bonjour Jeff – how about a waffle, non?" and we'd walk across the street.

I never ran into any of the problems I anticipated with a temperamental host. Antoine was fun guy and very easy to work with. On our final evening together, Antoine announced he had chartered a private yacht and invited us all out for a sunset cruise.

Antoine and I share a laugh on the yacht as the captain looks on.

Out in the Atlantic a school of dolphins joined us, leaping out of the water, keeping pace with the boat. We sailed up the coast, drinking and laughing and telling stories under the setting sun.

Dolphins leap of the coast of Virginia Beach beside our yacht.

The next day, the French contingent flew back to Europe and I was left to mix and edit the shows. It all went pretty much according to plan but, at one point during the audio mix, we ran into a snag.

It was an episode where Antoine had visited a remote Pacific island where he encountered a very rare bird. Antoine explained to the camera that this bird was unique since it made a sound like a small dog. But in the show the bird opened its mouth – and nothing came out. The sound was not on any of the tracks. We couldn't have him say that this rare bird sounded like a dog and then hear no sound.

I said to the audio engineer, "Get me a chihuahua and take out the bass."

He found a sound effect of a small dog, trimmed the equalizer and voila – *yip*. Perfect. The engineer just shook his head and joked, "If this was Nat Geo they'd have sent an audio crew back to the island."

I looked at him and smiled. Maybe Nat Geo would, maybe not. It certainly wasn't in my budget.

Today, with the internet giving us the world at our fingertips, I may have found that sound online. More likely, some wise guy who happened to have traveled to that remote island might just have called my bluff. But back then, it seems the audience was much more friendly and forgiving. No derogatory tweets or online attacks in 1998.

***

It is so much fun to write down these stories for my children. It's a rainy, dreary, overcast day in Berlin so I'm staying inside. I just cooked a full American breakfast – eggs, bacon, coffee and toast – and it feels like a touch of home. Days like this one seem slower than a normal day, a day when time has no meaning. Minutes turn into hours, hours turn into days.

I see commercials on TV portraying young couples in love. Most of my life I saw these as the present, possibly the future. Now I look at them and see my past, all the loves I've had, all those joys, my memories. When did that transition occur?

Looking out my window on the courtyard below, all is quiet. A low fog hangs silently over the city. Everything is silent except the soft patter of the rain. It seems like only yesterday I was a rising star at Discovery Channel. Boy, those were exciting times.

I close my eyes and think back...

***

By the time the year 2000 rolled around, I was a Senior Supervising Producer at Discovery and soon to become the Head of Reversioning for North America. Despite my old penchant for screwing up, I was gaining a reputation as a guy who could get things done.

See? Perseverance pays off. Don't let anyone ever tell you that you're not good enough. Don't listen to them. Never give up.

The energy at Discovery around this time was incredible. We were changing the world and we felt it. The hallways were buzzing with ideas and everything seemed possible.

Around this time networks like Fox and NBC were getting great ratings from shows that featured home video footage of people being rescued from fires, floods and various other disasters. Discovery wanted to get into the game and they located an existing thirteen half-hour series in New Zealand with a ton of great footage never seen in North America.

The problem was that the network feared possible press accusations of the Discovery Channel selling out its integrity for ratings. The Fox and NBC shows were full of 'eye candy,' the kind of video that makes the viewer stop and call someone else into the room to see it. The formula for the Fox and NBC shows tended to sensationalize the stories and exploit the victims.

The Discovery brass were afraid critics would accuse them of the same treatment. At that time, The Discovery Channel brand was the world leader for quality documentary television. The network felt the brand had to be protected at all costs. The brass were always nervous when something might possibly tarnish the brand.

I was called in to see Mike Quattrone, the head of Discovery Channel, to discuss the situation and whether we should pursue the project. Mike was firm. He told me in clear language to either come up with a way to pull it off with integrity or walk away from it.

I had been thinking about it in the days leading up to the meeting and suggested we feature the science and technology behind the rescues.

For example - what are the forces at work when a helicopter is pulling a victim out of a raging river? The river's current is pulling the victim downstream while the helicopter is pulling up. The chopper blades force air down and there is tension in the cable and a big change in resistance when the victim pops out of the water.

If we could graphically illustrate these principles we might have a solid show that would satisfy all concerned. I suggested we call the new Discovery series *Narrow Escapes*.

Quattrone liked my ideas and felt confident in me. Still, he wanted careful oversight of every aspect of the series as it unfolded. He made me the producer as well as the executive producer but he personally wanted to review every episode prior to air.

Mike was a cool character. He wasn't normally a micromanager. It was unusual to have the top guy at the network so involved but that's how sensitive he was to this content.

The competing networks had really milked the genre. The other programs showed clips of a dramatic rescue over and over, in slow motion, while wresting out the viewer's emotions. He wanted to make sure Discovery was held to a higher standard.

For extra insurance, Quattrone asked Steve Burns, Discovery's Head of Production, to be involved. Burns would review my rough cuts before I sent them to Quattrone.

I knew there would be a lot riding on my shoulders but as I left the meeting I felt like I was on top of the world. Even though my work would be scrutinized, even though the press might attack, even though the network's worldwide brand was on the line, they trusted me to craft this serious new primetime venture for the Discovery Channel. And I was confident I could do it.

I went off and came up with a budget, the biggest one I had ever crafted. Discovery had already negotiated a deal with the New Zealand production company that owned the original series for half a million dollars to own the rights in North America. The original series was thirteen half-hours.

Documentary networks like Discovery don't like half-hour shows as they're always hard-pressed to find a second half-hour series to pair along with them.

I figured I could use almost all the content and create six new hour-long shows. I knew I could use Discovery's in-house editing facilities, but I needed to budget for a freelance editor and graphics to help depict the science behind the rescues.

I also needed some help in the form of a trusted co-producer and associate producer. There would be some location shooting since I envisioned a new on-camera host and some additional interviews. But the big job of finding the unique rescue footage had already been done by the New Zealanders.

With Discovery already on the hook for half a million dollars for the footage, I estimated that I'd need another half million for my production costs, including travel. I typed up my budget and called another meeting with Quattrone.

As I went to sleep that night the gravity of the situation hit me. I was about to ask the Discovery Channel to trust me with six primetime hours of airtime, their brand-name reputation and a million dollars. Inside, I was still the guy who held Forrest Tucker's ashtray.

I better not fuck it up.

On the day of the meeting, my hands shook as I reached for Quattrone's doorknob. I felt a little dizzy and a lump rose in my throat. My sweaty palm slowly turned the door handle. I walked in and there was Quattrone with Steve Burns. I stood right in front of Quattrone's desk, tossed down my budget and looked him in the eye. As I did, I whispered to myself, "Do not blink."

Then I spoke.

Firmly I said, "It'll cost one million dollars."

Quattrone carefully poured over the numbers in my budget. As I stood there, heart pounding, his face offered no expression. I knew deep inside my budget was sound but the short time it took Quattrone to look over it felt like an eternity.

Finally, he looked up and said it looked OK to him but to let Steve Burns look at it then run it by one other senior executive.

Steve Burns looked at my budget even more carefully. It was buttoned up tight - a sound, reasonable budget with a reasonable shoot and edit schedule. No fat, only a small contingency fund for overages; basically, a good estimate of the expected costs.

"All the money will be on the screen," I added.

Burns gave me a nod of approval.

At that point I left Quattrone's office and collapsed in the stairwell. I couldn't believe he gave this former ashtray holder a million-dollar budget.

I only had one more hurdle before getting the green light. I was off to see the other senior exec.

This senior executive I needed to see was Danny Salerno. Danny had been around the company for a long time and had risen from the bottom to the top. He was known as the money man.

A down-to-earth guy with ice water in his veins, the day I walked into his office with my budget he hemmed and hawed awhile, talking about fiscal responsibility.

He was trying to rattle me, to see if everything in my figures were on the up-and-up.

"Every penny will be on the screen," I said.

I sat silently, waiting for his answer. After a deep breath and a long pause, he just nodded.

I got everything I asked for.

With the money in hand, I ordered the footage be sent from New Zealand and started to assemble my team.

I was lucky to get Pamela Deutsch as my co-producer. Deutsch and I were on the same level in the department and I asked her if she'd mind working for me for the duration of *Narrow Escapes*. She said she'd be thrilled and I was very happy to have someone so solid in the role to rely on.

Deutsch is a smart producer with a great attitude, a strong work ethic and a good sense of humor – just the right fit. We got along well. (It was a good thing as I would wind up working for her two years later on a series for the US National Parks.)

Julie Nadezna came aboard as my associate producer and the one person I could count on to mitigate my tendency to screw something up. Nadezna had extensive documentary writing credentials, experience working in tough locations around the world and had an amazing mind for detail. She became my right-hand.

With these two I felt I could accomplish just about anything, they were that good.

Backing us all up was the efficient, organized and reliable production assistant Deborah Ragan.

I knew we needed a good editor and all the ones I had worked with in the past were booked on other programs. Our editor on *Narrow Escapes* would often be working independently while the rest of us were off shooting so I knew we couldn't afford to get in trouble on this major multi-part series with a slow or disorganized editor.

A bad edit on a single hour-long documentary could often be salvaged but on a series, I needed a mature, reliable, creative editor - someone with real chops, someone clever who would be real value-added, someone who brought that something extra to the team.

Deutsch recommended Anne Goetz and, after interviewing her, I signed her right up. Smart, funny and multi-talented, Anne was just what we needed.

I've always tried to see beyond race and gender to choose crew members or narrators based solely on their skills and attitude. But it was pointed out to me that, unintentionally, I rounded out most of the rest of my staff with talented women.

We had good chemistry right from the start. For fun, my all-female team nicknamed themselves 'Jeff's Angels' and we set out to make a series that would do Discovery proud.

Kelly Phipps, Pamela Deutsch, Deborah Ragan, Lisa Dianna and Julie Nadezna
strike a pose as Jeff's Angels.

What luck I had pulling such a great team of people together and the fact that they were all available at the same time.

Over the course of a production, crew members spend many hours together. Each program I've embarked on had different requirements, unique needs and there is no single magic formula for success. Sometimes there are creative differences, budget problems, logistical issues, travel snafus, illnesses or family troubles and inevitably programs – especially documentaries – evolve as they move from concept through production on their way to the screen.

As with productions before, this crew would become a small temporary family and so much was riding on it. I wanted to get it right. When the hours get long, other commitments pull and tug, emotions can run high. I was very lucky to have this particular family to help me create the most important television series of my career.

I started creating the series by spending time with the New Zealand footage, watching it repeatedly, looking at the way the stories were told. The NZ show was simple: just show the event and maybe a short interview piece and then move on. The stories were cool and somebody was in the right place at the right time with a camcorder. There were spectacular mudslides, insane skiing accidents, animal rescues - all kinds of drama.

I made an index card of each story and pinned the cards to the wall of my office, a low tech but effective organizational method (much in the same way I eventually made cards for each story as I structured this book.)

I began to experiment, seeing how each episode of the new series might flow together, continually rearranging the cards.

Eventually the first five shows had some sort of cohesiveness. To tell them apart, each episode had a color associated with it. I didn't want to assign a number or suggest any type of order yet. I'd wait until they were finished and lead off with what I felt was the strongest episode.

The only problem early on was the sixth episode, the one labeled black, as in the black hole where all the crap that didn't fit ended up. It was a real hodge-podge of stories. I decided to worry about that one later.

This planning phase is called 'pre-production' – the part of the process where you're just conceptualizing before you pick up a camera. It is always a time of high enthusiasm.

It's also the part that most inexperienced producers tend to skip.

It's very tempting to jump right in and go shooting based on an initial idea. That is also the fastest way to burn up your budget and get stuck with less footage than you need at the end of a project.

Pre-production planning can be boring and frustrating but it's really the time when most of the creativity comes out. Ideas are tossed around. Plans change. Tangents are all run down. If these things happen after production starts it usually leads to money problems, stress and waste.

Running down all the possibilities early – before any big money is spent – is the best formula for success.

Alfred Hitchcock, the famed director and master storyteller, used to sketch his entire movie out in cartoon form before shooting anything. This way he ran down all the needs and possibilities before committing his crew. He once said he felt all the creativity was done before any of the film was shot.

For me, I like to plan as much as I can in advance. That way, I'm ready if it rains or if I see an opportunity arise during a shoot – like a spectacular sunset or a new interview subject – I'm ready, without causing my crew to work long days or busting my budget.

Every possible predictable element should get flushed out in pre-production. That investment in planning is worth every minute spent when you get a happy crew on location.

In my opinion, pre-production planning is the measure of a professional producer, someone who has really learned the trade, not just the tricks of the trade.

Soon I turned my attention to auditioning an on-camera host. I looked to my New York contacts but no one there really stood out. Refusing to settle, I decided to look west. I contacted a Hollywood talent agency and asked them to conduct a series of on-camera screen tests for me.

I told them I was looking for someone with good camera presence and some credibility with rescue situations. I wrote up some sample copy for them to read and waited. A few days later a stack of tapes arrived and I watched everyone's audition. A few were good and I made some notes.

Then I saw Michael Newman.

Newman's audition was off the charts. He was very casual and extremely confident. He seemed comfortable yet maintained a powerful presence in front of the camera. I found out later that the audition had taken place on his birthday and he was in a loose mood.

On the screen his look was tall and tough, but his delivery was cool and easy going. More importantly, he had some real-world credentials as a firefighter who jumped out of helicopters to fight forest fires as well as being a certified lifeguard and champion swimmer.

And he also had years of acting experience as Newmie, the only real lifeguard on the hit syndicated series *Baywatch*.

But he had something else. He had likeability. Like I often do with big decisions, I slept on it.

I signed Newmie up the next day and Michael Newman became the face of our series.

As the segments began to gel into some sort of show flow on my wall I wrote ins-and-outs. For *Narrow Escapes*, I envisioned the host on location, in environments similar to the storylines. Spending more time with the footage I determined we needed two basic geographic locations – one woodsy with streams and one exotic with beaches. I determined we could shoot locally in the Baltimore/Washington DC area for half of the stand ups.

For the other half, I chose Hawaii.

Once I had a firm grip on the flow of the first five episodes I gathered my producer and associate producer and the three of us watched the segments, discussed my ideas for ins and outs, moved around the index cards some more and the shows started to really transform from the New Zealand series into our Discovery Channel series.

We asked each other science questions about frostbite, G forces, aeronautics and more. Regan did some great fact checking and Nadezna began to take on some of the more bizarre ideas I came up with.

One exchange went like this:

"What if we had the narrator say a line then jump out of an airplane?" I asked.

"Well, he better get the line right the first time," she replied.

"And the audio will be terrible," I added. "But won't the shot look cool?"

"We could always try ADR."

ADR, or Automated Dialogue Replacement, is a film technique where the clean audio (usually the actor in a sound studio) replaces his or her lines by lip-synching.

It's often used when a scene is shot in a place that has loud or distracting extraneous noise. Most producers avoid ADR because it is both time consuming and often looks fake but it was a possibility.

"Let's just send him up, get the microphone in close and give it a try. We can always fix it in post," I smiled.

Everyone recognized the phrase. "Fix it in post" simply means to worry about it later.

Fortunately, we all had enough experience to have had real

nightmares in post-production and we knew we'd figure it all out *before* shooting began. We were still in the joyful, creative, optimistic pre-production phase so we just laughed.

We continued to plot out the storylines and brainstorm about locations. One shot envisioned the narrator on a Coast Guard boat, talking to the camera that was on another boat that was tracking alongside. We also had him doing stand ups in the middle of raging rapids, delivering a line from the back of a moving motorcycle, reading a line while surfing and doing a whole host of other wacky ideas.

Once I had a pretty good idea of the type of locations we wanted, I hired my old friend Larry to be the east coast location scout. Larry knew how to look for the right things, like where the sun is at certain times of the day and how much electricity is available on site. He also knew the area well.

But Larry's greatest asset was that I knew Larry was notoriously smart with a budget.

When you show up and say you're from The Discovery Channel and we want to shoot in your store, pool, yard or whatever, people tend to get dollar signs in their eyes. Larry knew we were on a budget and was used to getting things done without throwing around a lot of cash. And he had great attention to detail. He was the perfect location man.

Larry went out, took tons of photos, scouted the landscapes, made contacts, discussed availabilities and made sure we could get our catering truck in and out.

Known in the business as "craft services," this last detail was critical as a crew runs on food. The cost of a caterer is worth every penny. The last thing we needed was a grumpy bunch of hungry production people somewhere in the middle of a cold river.

If there is one lesson I could impart to any budding young producer it is that a well-cared for crew is a happy crew, and a happy crew makes happy TV shows. And they'll be loyal to you in the future. This is how reputations are made.

I've heard of cheap producers who try to squeeze every waking minute out of a crew with no care for their health or well-being. I'm on record right here that I think *they stink* - and give producer's everywhere a bad name.

That's one reason I feel a person should do every job on the crew before they become a producer. That way they know how to care for people. Too many producers and executive producers rise to the role without doing the other jobs first.

Like in most walks of life: take care of your people and they will take care of you.

One of my biggest challenges in the planning of *Narrow Escapes* was coming up with a real, workable shoot schedule.

Scenes are never shot in the order of their appearance in a show. If you have two shots by a river somewhere in the program, then you shoot them back to back. If they need to look like different times or places then you move the camera, get the host to change clothes, change the lighting, swap the props, whatever, but you shoot them back to back so you don't have to backtrack and waste time returning to a place you've already been.

One tip when drawing up a shoot schedule is that you never plan to do all your outdoor shooting, or 'exteriors,' at the end because it will surely rain or be the day someone decides to cut the grass and ruin the audio.

You try to stack the exteriors up front with a contingency plan each day for nearby interior shots if the weather or groundskeeper don't cooperate.

I assembled a list of east coast props I wanted — a Mack truck, a helicopter, a wetsuit - and gave it to Nadezna.

Availability would dictate some of the schedule and I needed to know what I could get and when. I also had to calculate travel time between locations, where the sun would be at a given time of day and estimate how long each shot would take.

A good shoot schedule is the blueprint, the foundation upon which everything else is built. Time is money so building a schedule too loose wastes resources. Building one too tight is a fast way to tension on location.

Once we had our shoot schedule it was time to bring in a crew. On Pam's recommendation I hired Frank Maniglia as camera operator and his audio guy David Schmidt for the east coast portion. We also contracted Doug Drew, a freelance jib operator.

A 'jib' is a long pole, often 30 or 40 feet, that the camera attaches to with remote controls. It was the way to get those sweeping shots that come down from the trees before drones. Even today, drones are too noisy for narrations.

For this shot the jib would smoothly glide the camera over the top of the helicopter then rest it on Newmie as he delivered his lines. Note the heavy counterweights on the back of the jib to balance out the load.

I also hired Rhett Bloomquist as my lighting director, an area veteran I'd known for years, another one of those guys committed to doing whatever was necessary.

There is an old saying about lighting guys. They like to tweak and tweak, trying to get things perfect for each set up while everyone sits around waiting, burning up so much time and money that you eventually have to slap them and shout, "It's good enough!"

I knew Rhett was skilled and efficient at working fast – a good combination – and I never had to wait long for his set ups. And, as a former lighting director myself, I could appreciate what he was striving for.

With a reliable crew and a new Discovery credit card I was ready to roll.

I flew in Michael Newman from the west coast and put him up in a nice hotel with arrangements to have him picked up in the morning for our first day of location shoots. Deutsch arranged for the energetic Kelly Phipps, a freelance producer, to be Mr. Newman's driver. She was over qualified but had a lot of fun with the role.

For our first location my friend Jimmy Eicholtz had told me about a fire fighter's training academy. It was a cool location with props rigged with gas jets that could send out twenty-foot flames on command.

The east coast crew for *Narrow Escapes* with firefighters from the Maryland Fire & Rescue Institute who helped out that day. Far left: lighting director Rhett Bloomquist. Back row, to the right of the camera: audio guy David Schmidt, camera operator Frank Maniglia, Newmie, production assistant Deborah Ragan, make-up artist Lisa Dianna, me, gaffer Frank Caslin. Front row, second from left: Kelly Phipps (AKA Mr. Newman's Driver.) Front row center, kneeling: location scout Larry Bowers, producer Pam Deutsch, associate producer Julie Nadezna. These people are some of the members of the best production team I ever assembled.

At our disposal we had a burning three-story building, a giant tanker truck that would burst into flames and a slew of fire fighters to rush in as extras, spraying fire hoses whenever we wanted.

The very first shot had no flames but it did call for Newmie to rappel down the side of a building.

Newmie rappels down a nine-story building for a stand up as the crew looks on from below.

He'd be wearing a wireless microphone, giving his lines as he plummeted. We got him to the top and he stepped off for a rehearsal. He huffed and puffed his lines all the way down and the audio guy gave me the headphones for playback. The heavy breathing wasn't what we were after.

I decided Newmie should just step out over the edge, rappel down into the shot, read his lines to the camera, and then drop down out of the shot. We sent Newmie back to the top and he stepped off but while we were repositioning the camera he lost his footing and was now dangling upside down a hundred feet from the ground.

I thought I was going to kill him on the very first shot.

Fortunately, after a tense few moments, he righted himself and we got a beautiful shot with bright blue skies and big puffy white clouds behind him.

The giant burning tanker truck was a great prop and I felt compelled to use it. It was one of those times when I got to a location, saw an unforeseen opportunity and knew my shoot schedule so well that I could shift things around and not get into trouble.

The shot I envisioned had our jib fly up and over the flames then come down to reveal Newmie emerge from a thick cloud of black smoke. We tried shot after shot, but the wind kept changing and the raging fire kept sending waves of smoke toward the camera, obscuring the shot. Newmie was gagging but he hung in there and we eventually got a take we could use before we asphyxiated him.

Frank Maniglia looks on as Newmie prepares his stand up in front of the burning tanker. The large square things are reflectors used to pump sunlight in where desired.

We shot in and around Maryland for about a week – in a stream, on a horse farm, anywhere it made sense to introduce one of the stories.

With half of the stand-ups in the can, Newmie and I set off for Hawaii. The plan was to pick up a local crew on location.

Picking up a local crew is a risk because you're putting your faith in people you've never worked with before but the budget saves on transportation and lodging plus you get the benefit of working with locals who know their way around.

In Honolulu, Newmie and I got suites at the Hilton Hawaiian Village, right on the beach at Waikiki. He was familiar with the place as it was his home-away-from-home while shooting on location for *Baywatch*. I hired Marilyn Mick, an Oahu-based location manager to make all our Hawaii arrangements. She brought in Ken Libby as camera operator and Libby brought his favorite audio guy.

On our first morning we were on the east side of Oahu on a beautiful stretch of beach. We got there before daybreak and at dawn a golden sun emerged over the blue Pacific. The shot looked fantastic and we began to tape Newmie's stand up in that honey-colored morning light. I thought it would look cool if Newmie had a parrot on his shoulder and had arranged for an animal handler to bring one.

We had a track constructed on the beach and the camera moved along on the track with Newmie as he spoke. Each time we rolled, Newmie would stop before he completed his lines and we had to go back and reset the shot.

He had been so smooth with his delivery on the east coast so I didn't understand why he kept muffing his lines take after take. Finally, after a dozen takes, we got one where Newmie managed to speak all his lines. Afterward, the handler took the bird off his shoulder and Newmie sat down next to me. He pulled off his shirt and showed me why he had such a problem delivering his lines. He was bleeding where the parrot had dug eight little holes in his shoulder with its talons.

Newmie's kept his personal cigarette boat at a marina in Honolulu and one day we took it out for a stand up. This thing was long, lean and very fast.

During a break, he said it felt like there was some seaweed stuck on the propeller. Without notice, my narrator leapt off the boat and disappeared beneath it. The crew and I sat looking at one another with puzzled looks. He was down there a long time. If he didn't surface soon we were not only without a narrator, we were without someone who knew how to drive the boat.

After two long minutes Newmie popped up holding a handful of seaweed.

I learned early on in my career that one thing all seasoned producers try to do when traveling to exotic locations is to build at least one weekend into the shoot schedule to have some time off while the lodging is still picked up by the production budget.

On Friday night, Newmie and I were enjoying a few drinks at the hotel's Shell Bar, relaxing after a long week of work. We were happy. We knew we were getting good stuff on tape and the weekend loomed. We told a few stories, had a few laughs then I felt like turning in.

As I got up to leave Newmie said, "Hey, want to go for a paddle tomorrow morning?"

Not sure what he meant but thinking about a little exercise rowing a canoe I said, "Sure."

"Great," he added. "Meet me at my suite at 7:00 AM."

Half lit and happy I just waved and left for my room.

The next morning, still unsure of what I'd gotten myself into, I knocked on Newmie's door at 7:00. Newmie, at six-foot-four, dwarfed me as he opened the door and handed me an oar.

Still unsure of what I was in for, we walked down to a secluded spot behind the hotel where Newmie took the cover off a twelve-foot sea kayak. I call it a kayak but you couldn't get into it. It was more like a long pointed tube you wrap your legs around.

"It's a *Baywatch* prop but they let me use it," he beamed as we dragged it from its hiding place.

Sure enough the long red kayak had the *Baywatch* logo emblazoned on its side.

Clumsily I managed to help him carry the thing down to the tranquil still waters of the lagoon. Here he showed me how to sit, paddle and get on and off the thing. The water was as smooth as glass and with a little effort I managed to stay on the long, unwieldy, hard-plastic tube long enough for Newmie to declare me fit to accompany him on a paddle.

We paddled across the lagoon, him on the front, me at the back with about four feet of tube between us. I was glad I was in the back as I wasn't sure how long I could keep pace with the athletic lifeguard. I should say here that not only had I never kayaked before, I was grossly out of shape - a doughy blob of white, untanned skin on the back of a red tube wearing prescription eyeglasses. My pasty physique must've stood out in strong contrast to the tall, tan and lean Newmie to anyone out for a morning stroll that day.

When we safely reached the other side of the lagoon I felt a deep sigh of relief. I'd managed to stay on the damn thing and keep pace although I was a little winded.

"We can put in over there," he said, pointing to the beach.

"Put in?"

"Yeah, you know. To the ocean."

Good God, this man expects me to ride this red plastic tube in the Pacific Ocean?

I looked at him dead pan for an instant. He just smiled and I realized at that moment that I'd almost killed him a few times already during this shoot. Now this was his turn to try and kill me.

I knew I needed to maintain a good relationship with my narrator and I told him I'd do this. After all, he couldn't do it by himself. What the hell? I'd come this far. I decided to suck it up and picked up my end of the tube and we made for the shore.

At the water's edge, Newmie pointed out that the waves were breaking so many meters out and we'd need to head straight into them to avoid capsizing. He climbed aboard the front of the tube and angled it toward the waves.

The waves coming off the Pacific Ocean at Waikiki were fucking big. Reluctantly, I straddled the back end as Newmie dug in his oar and we were off. Soon we slammed head-on into the blasting, relentless waves.

As we rode over them I just put my head down, squeezed my legs around the tube and paddled for my life. The long tube tipped high, raising the front as Newmie's body blocked the horizon. Then it slammed down, raising the back end up high.

My legs tightened even more around the giant plastic tube as I risked sliding off into the sea. It was at this moment that I asked myself an all too familiar question, "What the hell am I doing here?"

But I had no time to ponder as the nose of the tube pointed back toward the sky.

I saw Newmie lean forward, the way a rider does on a horse that jumps over a fence and quickly decided it would be a good idea for me to lean forward too. I did and the long tube slapped back down on the surface of the water, pressing the hard-plastic *Baywatch* prop firmly into my face. I bounced back up like a punching bag, stopping myself from falling off by the manic need to paddle as fast as I possibly could.

Soon we were out of the breakers and onto the open ocean. Newmie kept paddling like he was trying to break a speed record. I kept paddling because I was scared shitless, moving on pure adrenaline.

We kept this up until I was spent with exhaustion. Sensing I had stopped paddling Newmie also stopped and we sat quietly on the giant red tube out in the middle of the ocean. Over his shoulder he asked how I was doing. I was unable to speak as I had no energy left after the exhausting wave battering and the endless paddling.

Slowly the tube drifted around in a circle. Diamond Head, the large rock formation to the east of Waikiki, came into view from an angle I'd never seen before. It was also a lot smaller than I'd remembered it.

As the tube bobbed around in the water I could see more of the coast, then finally Waikiki Beach where we put in. My mouth dropped open as the buildings seemed about two inches tall. We were so far out!

As the amazement of what we'd done dawned on me, Newmie jumped off the front of the tube and into the sea. Popping up he said, "Let's see how you do on your own." "What?!" I stammered.

I moved my oar ever so slightly and upset my fragile center of balance. Almost immediately I fell off the slippery tube and splashed like a rock into the sea.

As the cool waters of the deep Pacific enclosed around me cutting off my senses, I instinctively reached up and caught my prescription eyeglasses just before they fell to the ocean floor. Sputtering and flailing, I burst back to the surface.

I clung to the side of the long red tube and wondered how I'd ever manage to possibly haul myself back onto the stupid thing. By this time, Newmie was laughing out loud while he bobbed blissfully between the waves.

Mercifully, he jumped back on and held the kayak firm as I desperately scrambled onto its back.

Once we were both aboard he indicated that we should go around Diamond Head and explore. As we did, he paddled like a piston. Happy to be in the back and out of sight, I maintained a somewhat steady but much less enthusiastic pace.

Drenched and spent, I tried to take in the scenery while keeping my terror disguised from Newmie.

Eventually we came back around and thankfully started to make our way back toward Waikiki Beach. Newmie pointed toward some pilings, a row of large thick wooden poles that formed two columns. "We need to go between those pilings. That channel will ensure we don't run up on a sand bar," he shouted back at me.

I nodded and then frantically paddled with all the little strength I had left as we made for the channel. If knew that if I could just get back to that beach I'd survive.

The skyline grew larger each time I glanced up from my rowing. Dear

God, it looks like we're gonna make it.

But my optimism was short-lived for, just as we entered the narrow channel between the pilings, a rogue wave came from our left and knocked the kayak over on its side. I saw Newmie fly off the front. His head appeared to hit one of the large wooden pilings and he disappeared under the waves.

"Good God," I thought, "am I going to have to *save* him?"

I somehow managed to stay on the tube gripping it with my legs in a death choke. The wave then threw the tube back up and it quickly righted itself. The front end flew up toward the sky without Newmie's weight on it. I scanned the breakers but could not see him. My mind flooded with questions.

"Where the hell is he?"

"Is he dead?"

"How am I going to drag him ashore? He's huge!"

"What will I tell the network?"

"Will insurance cover stupidity?"

"Do I really have to rescue the lifeguard? How ironic is that?"

Just then Newmie popped up, grasped the front of the tube, slid back on and we rode in on the next powerful wave, our oars following behind us.

I washed up on shore like a refugee, out of breath, bedraggled, looking like a drowned rat. My solace at the feel of sand beneath my feet was broken by a huge round of applause. I looked up to see that a crowd of about a hundred people had gathered, apparently intrigued by the Baywatch prop - and they recognized Michael Newman. Newmie took a bow as I passed out and fell backwards onto the soft sand of Waikiki Beach.

The rest of the shooting went smoothly after Newmie's reciprocal near-death paddle idea.

We did the shot with him on the Coast Guard boat as well as surfing and more but I didn't have him jump out of a plane. I took one look at the plane we'd arranged for and it looked like it was literally on its last flight, barely held together with twine and gaffers tape. We shot Newmie's stand up while he stood next to it.

When we finished taping in Hawaii I brought the tapes back home for editing. The magic happens in the edit suite and our editor was really making it all work.

Goetz had already dropped in the east coast stand ups along with our new graphics, the new science material and style elements. Adding the Hawaii footage, the series was really taking shape.

I approved some rough cuts and began my reviews with the network executives. I got great feedback. After some minor changes five episodes had a good feel except the black one, the dumping ground for all the segments that didn't quite fit.

What did these segments all have in common? A bozo jumps cars and crashes. Another bozo jumps stuff on a motorcycle and crashes. A daredevil buried himself alive in a Plexiglas box that burst under the weight of the soil. These were all... what – idiots?

I'd recently read a magazine article about a psychiatrist who specialized in adrenaline junkies and thought that idea just might be the thread - adrenaline junkies. How about an interview with the psychiatrist from the article who'll comment on their behavior?

I contacted the doctor and asked Deutsch to interview him. She did, and we edited the psychiatrist's comments in seamlessly. The black hole now had a theme. The series was complete and the network approved the roughs. I sent the edited masters off to Jeff Order who composed a magnificent original score for the series and Craig Maniglia did the final mix. Finally, after a great experience, I delivered the series.

The promo department scored a coup when they floated an advance copy of the series to Oprah Winfrey. Her producers liked both the drama of *Narrow Escapes* and the science behind the rescues. Oprah devoted an entire episode of her talk show to it. After interviewing some of the people profiled in *Narrow Escapes* and showing their dramatic rescues, I'll never forget how she turned to the camera and told the audience that this was quality television. She implored everyone to tune into *Narrow Escapes*.

I couldn't have been prouder.

When the series debuted on Discovery primetime, *Narrow Escapes* led the night in ratings every time it aired. There was never the backlash the network feared as the critics also loved it.

As for me, I felt I'd really hit the big time.

It wasn't yet a documentary entirely of my own design, the one I dreamed of years earlier on my parent's couch, the one I envisioned while sitting on the owl, but I now had real credibility.

I was closing in on my mountaintop.

6

I am up at dawn, watching Berlin wake up.

As I walk I notice that most of the shops aren't open yet but I see the shopkeepers inside getting ready for their day. They seem to move briskly, less a frenetic fury, more a sane measured intent.

Café Cinema is closed but I find the Starbucks open and order a small breakfast. I sit in the window and watch the people of Berlin. A yellow tram slows to a stop in front of me. The doors slide open and passengers climb aboard, off to work, to life. The doors close, a little red light flashes and the tram glides away into the city.

Across the street an old man is standing on the sidewalk smoking a meerschaum pipe bursting great puffs of white smoke into the air as schoolboys with leather boxes strapped to their backs run toward school.

Out of the blue a beautiful blonde woman appears. She was buying a coffee. I must have been writing as I did not see her enter the Starbucks but as she pulls the door to leave she turns toward me, looks into my eyes, smiles, pauses ever so slightly and whispers, "Morgen," or 'good morning' in German and quietly warms my heart.

When I finish my coffee and leave the coffee shop I look for her.

She has vanished but her gesture remains with me for a while.

I wander north in my neighborhood to a used clothing store on the Schönhauser Allee. I like to visit thrift shops and flea markets when I travel as they are often a great source for props, costumes and period clothing. Plus, it's just another form of recycling.

Inside I see a collection of castoffs, each with their own little story. There are soccer shirts, formal gowns, pieces of traditional German costumes. A rack of long black leather overcoats lines one entire wall, mobile shelters from the cold Berlin winter. I look around but I exit the shop without buying anything. I have enough memories of my own right now.

As I walk across town I look again for the woman who smiled at me. The only face I see for a second time today is the old man with the pipe.

Across the street I see two young lovers embrace. The young man has his back to me. He has a messenger bag hanging from his shoulder as do half of the men in Berlin. I can see the woman's face for a moment. I see her expression and understand. She looks emotionally moved, speechless, and very happy. It is the kind of moment people want to lock in their hearts and remember. It is love. Soon they reel away and disappear into the crowd down the cobblestone streets of Berlin lined with motionless bicycles patiently waiting to take their owners on another local journey.

In another winter the woman I was in love with sat next to me under a blanket in a horse-drawn carriage in Central Park in New York City. My heart pounded as I felt for the little white box in my pocket.

We got out at the Angel of the Waters Fountain and walked down to the water's edge. While she sat on a bench I got down on one knee and asked her to marry me.

She clasped her hands to her face, drew in a deep breath and through tear soaked eyes looked down and said yes. That night we had a happy dinner with friends, made a spate of hurried phone calls, posted our joy-filled photos to Facebook and collapsed into one another's arms in the hidden confines of a small hotel off Washington Square.

The story might have ended there but it was a short-lived bliss. By spring our paths had begun to drift.

In summer we paused and thought and paused and thought again. And before the first leaf in autumn fell we had parted.

Now it is winter again and I am alone. The airline ticket that brought me here was purchased with the intent to whisk us both off to a Honeymoon on the sunny Amalfi Coast. But instead I used it to go to Berlin.

And now I am by myself under the heavy grey winter skies. It is a very different trip.

I'm taking little pieces of my history, holding them up to the light and writing them down.

And my heart is resting on the plateau between loves. It's a good reason to spend some time alone.

I'm taking the U-Bahn to the flea market on Boxhagener Platz.

Walking through the neighborhood approaching the Platz, the golden sun is dappled on the cobblestones by bare tree branches. Arriving at the market I see that the vendors are still setting up shop. The crunching of their footsteps on the gravel is woven under the sound of an old gypsy woman playing violin on the corner.

I slip into the small stream of early shoppers slowly walking through the half-empty stalls. I'm having trouble focusing. I'm lonely and I need to push through it.

All the objects for sale have a past but few speak to me.

Then I see a grey coat and slip it on. It fits well and feels like an old friend so I buy it. Leaving the market, I cross the street to a cafe for a second cup of coffee. Sitting at a little table outside I wish the old grey coat could talk and tell me where it's been.

I fish through the pockets for a clue and find a small stone in the shape of a heart. It is in the breast pocket, over my own heart. How did the previous owner obtain it? Was it a gift from a lover to remember her by?

The stone heart is smooth in my fingers. It has brightened my mood, reminding me that there is love in the world. I don't feel lonely anymore.

The stone, moments after I discovered it, next to my notebook.

Pulling the grey coat tighter against the cold I see my reflection in the cafe window, a transparent image that is temporary and when it's gone it will leave no trace. I look at my face and wonder how many years I have left.

As I write my parents are still alive. Dad is 92 and legally blind but his mind is still razor sharp. Mom is 89. Her bootlegger mother lived to be 95. The odds are pretty good that I'll live a long time.

I think about what it would be like to retire here in Berlin. Looking down I realize that the uneven cobblestones would be difficult for an old man to navigate. And the Berlin winter is probably too cold.

I smile because I know it doesn't matter.

I've never been good at predicting the future.

And today is about remembering the past.

***

l have had many experiences and opportunities through the years. I attribute it to the ability to stumble through doors, risk embarrassment, make mistakes, learn from them and never give up.

Through it all I still had one eye on my mountaintop, that personal goal I made sitting on the owl. I still wanted to create an original program of my very own from scratch, a show that aired coast-to-coast.

Soon I had completed *Top Ten National Parks to See Wildlife* for my *Narrow Escapes* cohort Pam and the Travel Channel. I also made a show from California fire footage for TLC. Both were new shows but crafted from existing material.

I was developing some momentum.

Now I wanted to take my shot.

Sometime around this period I'd also renarrated a French production on volcanoes featuring the exquisite cinematography and photographs of the late Maurice and Katia Kraftt. During my research I'd come across the work of a gifted camera operator named Mick Kalber and saw his incredible footage of the Kilauea Volcano in Hawaii.

I did a little more research and came up with a new show idea. Even though my department had never created an original, I knew it was time to try and break new ground.

I worked up a budget and pitched my idea to the Travel Channel for a new documentary I called *Best Place to Watch a Volcano.*

The pitch session was full of people who knew what I could deliver. There was a mutual respect in the room, but this would be far from a free pass.

Networks get pitched so many ideas and so few get made - something between one and two percent. Plus, my department had never made anything totally from scratch before.

I knew had to be on my game.

I showed them Mick Kalber's footage, discussed the concept, presented my ideas and waited. After a few closed-door meetings without me, I got the call.

The Travel Channel really liked my pitch. They gave me the green light and authorized my budget. I would be the producer and report to Cathryn Garland as my executive producer.

I was excited. I got into pre-production mode and the creativity machine switched into high gear.

This was my chance to make a real documentary of my very own that would air not only coast to coast but all over the world. I did months of pre-production planning.

I'm particularly proud of one sequence and it was totally conceived during the pre-production phase. I learned that lava is around 2000 degrees Fahrenheit, roughly four times as hot as your backyard barbecue, roughly one fifth the temperature of the surface of the sun.

I wanted to illustrate these facts and put that heat into context. I used this sequence as a transition from the lava flow to an interview with a helicopter pilot discussing the dangers of flying over an active volcano.

Here's how I sketched out the sequence:

Close up of lava

Dissolve to close up of barbecue with a steak on the grill

Hand flips steak to hear the sizzle

Narrator compares the barbeque temps to lava temps

Wide shot of our Hawaiian actress flipping the steak

Close up of her cool drink with a round lemon slice on the rim

Narrator remarks on the refreshment of a cool drink on a hot day then compares lava to the temperature of the surface of the sun

Dissolve to the sun, in the same place on the screen as the lemon slice, as the silhouette of a helicopter emerges from the center of the sun and banks right

Cut to an overhead shot of the helicopter on the ground, blades spinning, pilot in cockpit

Dissolve to a high shot above a spinning ceiling fan with the pilot we're interviewing in a chair exactly where pilot was in the helicopter

Begin his interview under the shot

Cut to close up of pilot

Now we're into the interview

During pre-production I spoke to Mick Kalber by phone many times. We flushed out ideas, lined up some interviews - including the one with the pilot - arranged for a crew, props and an actress, scripted an opening title sequence and put together a shoot schedule.

Meanwhile I had a ceiling fan shipped to his home so we could get one of the shots in that sequence.

Mick would play many key roles during the Hawaii leg of the production. He scouted locations, arranged for the helicopter, talked to Park Ranger Jeff Judd – a man who once was engulfed in flames at a lava flow – and convinced Judd to give me an exclusive on-camera interview.

Then Mick pitched me this idea. "How about we shoot a real wedding out on the lava flow?" asked Mick.

"Sounds cool. Whose wedding?" I asked.

"Mine," Mick replied.

Mick had thought long and hard about marrying his longtime

girlfriend, Annie, and this show offered an opportunity. I was looking for unusual angles for the program. If I picked up the tab for the helicopter that was needed to shuttle the wedding party, the cake, and the minister out to the lava flow, we could use his story in our show.

"Let me think about it," I replied.

I called Mick back the next day and told him we could do it but I needed to set a few conditions.

Mick often worked as a camera operator for network affiliated TV stations. I told Mick that if he would offer the footage of the wedding to a station, and that station agreed to offer it to the rest of their network affiliates, *and* we could have the words COURTESY OF THE TRAVEL CHANNEL burned onto the screen, then we would put the wedding on our shoot schedule. Mick would have to send his own wedding footage to TV stations around the country. He agreed.

Soon I found myself on a plane to The Big Island of Hawaii. I flew into Kona, spent the night, then drove my Jeep down around the southern tip of the island and over to Hilo where I met up with Mick Kalber.

Upon my arrival in Hilo, I went to dinner with Mick and Annie. They were excited about the show, their own wedding, and we had a lot of details to work out. We sat down in a little pasta bar and, as we spoke, people kept dropping by the table to say hello. It seemed Mick and Annie knew the entire town. Mick's work had been seen around the world and he was a local celebrity. Add Annie's infectious charm and it was little wonder people were drawn to them.

Getting a good angle for volcano watching was pretty much Mick's job. He'd been chasing eruptions for the better part of two decades and had emerged as one of the world's leading photographers on volcanic activity. His workplace was *hot*. One time while shooting, his camera began to melt. Here was Mick's description of working near such intense heat.

"I've melted a lot of things out there. I used to wear tennis shoes because they didn't retain the heat and would cool off quickly when I got off the hot stuff but, unfortunately, tennis shoes melt when they get too hot. I've stood in a lot of places out there that would melt anything. You have to watch where you put things. I've melted lens shades, parts of cameras, tripod feet, and backpacks - all kinds of things."

We'd have to be careful when we went out. We also had to plan on a lot of possible alternate shoots due to inclement weather. Hilo is the rainiest spot in the in the US. It rains nearly every day, but that belies the real beauty of the place. The rain is gentle and the sun still shines, creating an unbelievable daily display of spectacular rainbows.

We busted out our shoot schedule and hit the ground running. The next thing I knew, I was in a helicopter landing next to a bubbling, unpredictable volcano shooting lava out in every direction. It was an incredible experience - to see the birth of new land and to feel the kind of heat that melts rocks.

On the volcano, a strange feeling came over me. Me. Father of two, sedan-driving, mutual fund-buying, throw-the-milk-out-after-it-expires, me. Not exactly your classic risk-taker.

Suddenly, I found myself standing on a hot, black surface – the newest land on earth – as I stared at red-hot molten lava gushing violently into the sea.

The ground all around me was burning and the white-hot steam shot high into the sky over my head. I could feel the power of the earth itself as the ground rumbled and shook.

My heart began to pound wildly and that little familiar voice inside once again asked, "What the hell am I doing here?"

But then, gradually, a steadier calm descended on me. This was *pretty cool*. Hey, I knew anything could happen and yet, there I stood, on the edge of an active volcano.

We got a few shots, scouted the location for the wedding and soon our work was done and I was back in the helicopter. As the helicopter lifted off and the blades chopped through the hot heavy air, I could feel my legs shaking as if I'd just cheated death once again.

I envisioned a complicated title sequence with a *Lara Croft, Tomb Raider* type of actress running through the jungle while native drummers pounded out the beat before a giant volcano erupts exploding out the show's title.

I carefully storyboarded each shot, hired a stunning actress for the role, brought in three huge Polynesian guys and had an artist paint them up with symbols. Three drums were rented from a shop on the north shore of the island and we selected a spectacular location by a remote waterfall.

We shot those scenes on a Friday and the rented drums needed to be returned the next day. The deal involved some store credit upon return and I offered to return them thinking I could come back with souvenirs for the family purchased with the store credit.

I was given the drums and an address in a small town named Kapa'au near the top end of The Big Island. The next day, Saturday, was a day off so I packed the drums into my rented Jeep and set out for Kapa'au. I thought, "How far could it be? After all, I'm on an island."

Due to volcanic activity, the primary road north was impassable. To make matters worse, my rental car agreement forbade me to drive on the Saddle Road that bisected the island since, for a long time, this road was considered the most dangerous road in the state, with many rough areas and marginally maintained pavement. No, I would have to drive from Hilo in the east, south around the coast, then back up the west side of the island to reach Kapa'au on the north shore.

What should've been about an hour-and-a-half drive to get there turned into a five-hour ordeal. They don't call it The Big Island for nothing.

At one point I drove along a high mountain ridge where a steady wind bent all the trees down sideways. With nothing between me and 6,000 miles of open ocean, the wind seemed determined to blow both me and my Jeep off the mountain. I think I was on that damn ridge for over an hour.

Then I drove through a pine forest. That, too, seemed to go on endlessly. Still, no sign of Kapa'au. I kept thinking, "Where the hell is this place?!"

After stopping for meals, gas and leg stretches, I literally drove *all day* before finally finding this tiny town on the north shore around dusk. I returned the drums, traded them for a few T-shirts, trinkets and a CD by a local Native American flute player I'd met named Troy De Roche and set out for the long drive back to my hotel.

I'd lost the entire day and most of the night. When I phoned home, I joked with my children that Kapa'au was the one place in the world I'd never return to *because it's just too far.* To this day that's how the town is referred to by my family.

My next drive would be even more bizarre. The day of the wedding I set out to meet the chopper alone, in my Jeep, with a hand-drawn map from Mick.

As advised I steered the Jeep off the main road and sped down a two-lane highway where the street signs direct you toward Kalapana. Twenty miles later, at the end of a lonely stretch of blacktop far from civilization, the road ended before me.

As it turns out, the entire town of Kalapana was wiped out by a massive volcanic flow a little over 10 years earlier. Now, beyond a small wooden barrier, all that remained was a black abyss. The lava bed had consumed the area entirely. My instructions were to drive over the lava bed three times - until I came to the third stretch of old highway. That's where the helicopter would land and pick me up.

Driving over a lava field is a slow and jarring experience.

I slipped the Jeep into four-wheel drive and headed into the vast unknown. The ride was bumpy and slow-going.

The hot sun bore down on the shade-less landscape and I could see enormous waves of heat as they rose up all around me. The rugged sheet of jagged, volcanic rock revealed few clues about the entombed landscape beneath it. After about ten minutes, the highway emerged again and I was speeding along, completely alone, on a road to nowhere.

Fifteen minutes later I came upon the second lava flow, even bumpier than the first. I began to question the directions. In the far distance I could see the giant steam cloud rising where the active lava meets the ocean.

With no cell phone coverage, I couldn't call and check in with Mick, so I simply pressed on, ever slowly, over the volcanic ruts and rocks toward the next stretch of highway.

After another half-hour, the highway appeared again and while driving on it, I felt like a time traveler. To my right were some houses eerily left untouched by the lava. They were now totally isolated in a volcanic wilderness. To my left was the Pacific Ocean, an endless expanse of brilliant blue.

The third and final lava flow I had to cross was the most treacherous – a rollicking ride that strained the undercarriage of the Jeep and tossed me around like a lottery ball before the big drawing.

"Why couldn't the damn helicopter meet me at the first stretch of highway?" I mused, while trying to separate my spleen from colon. "Surely the Saddle Road couldn't have been worse than this," I thought.

After inching my way across the last harrowing expanse of volcanic cliffs and ditches, I finally arrived at what I believed would be the meeting point. As it turns out, from the air it's rather easy to spot a disheveled producer in a white Jeep in a vast black wasteland.

The big gray helicopter swooped in, collected me and whisked me off to the wedding, which was in a remote spot where the lava meets the sea. No cars could reach it. The entire wedding party - including bridesmaids, flower girl, champagne and all - had to be ferried in via chopper.

The helicopter also came in handy when it was discovered that Annie's wedding dress had been accidentally left behind in Hilo.

As a rule, you need a USGS geologist in your party to land a helicopter out where the lava is flowing and geologist Jim Kauahikawa attended the wedding. Visitors need to be very careful where they step. What looks like solid rock can really be a thin crust over molten lava.

Even with all the proper precautions, Jim's expert guidance and Mick's experience, the wedding party still couldn't avoid the pounding heat and searing fumes. With the hot black earth reflecting the pounding sun all around us, three people fainted during the ceremony.

But the volcano cooperated, steadily, but safely, sending a steam cloud fifteen hundred feet above our heads as the red-hot lava shot into the cold ocean. In fact, the ceremony was beautiful. At the end of the day, we'd gotten the shots, the wedding was official, the cake was a hit, and everyone left giddy and unscathed.

Shooting the wedding on the lava flow for *Best Place to Watch a Volcano*. The steam in the background marks the spot where molten lava is entering the Pacific Ocean.

The wild volcanic backdrop for the wedding was just outside the southeast border of Hawaii Volcanoes National Park. No one had bothered to inform the volcano to please stay inside the park's boundaries. This raging, erupting landscape was in sharp contrast to the sedate confines of the park's large visitor's center.

One hundred yards behind the visitor's center, in a ramshackle supply closet filled with hundreds of pieces of high-tech lifesaving gear, I met up with Jeff Judd. Jeff comes off as a mild-mannered unassuming Park Ranger, but he has a wild past.

To look at him, you wouldn't imagine this is a guy who has stared down death not once, but multiple times.

In an earlier career Jeff was a geologist. One sunny afternoon he was flying over Kilauea doing a survey of the park when suddenly the chopper in which he was flying with two others experienced catastrophic engine failure.

"For whatever reason," he recalled, "the gearbox failed, or exploded. We were coming in for a landing and turned over in the air. We crashed upside down and tumbled across the lava flow for about 100 yards. It knocked all of us out. Next thing I knew I woke up and the aircraft is upside down with the engine still running - no blades, just this screaming turbine noise. We all got out of it alive, fortunately. But when helicopters crash, you never know what will happen."

Jeff Judd's accident occurred far from the active flow that day so they were in no danger of falling into hot lava. But that wasn't his only brush with disaster.

In a separate incident, Jeff *did* fall into hot lava and is one of the few people to live to tell about it.

One afternoon Jeff was taking some volcanic samples at a spot he had visited countless times before. He was just a few feet away from a river of molten lava when he tried to get a fresh sample with a small hammer. It was a tough memory for him to recall. Reluctantly he told me what happened.

"I stepped onto what I thought was hard rock – and I sank right through. At the same time, my momentum was pitching me forward into the river. Here I am, on fire, the lava burning my boot and jeans, my skin, my leg – flames roaring up my body – and I'm pitching forward into this river.

"All I could do was throw my hammer to the side and get some momentum to spin around and fall back. My hands went into a very red hot glowing crack on the side of a cinder cone. I pulled myself out and sat there for a minute in disbelief."

Jeff Judd was literally on fire that day but he has fully recovered from his injuries. His hands have healed but the skin on his leg remains pale and soft, unable to grow hair.

Today he makes a living rescuing others. He lives in Volcano Village, just outside Hawaii Volcanoes National Park. It's the closest town to the Kilauea Volcano, but he wouldn't consider moving to safer ground. Regardless of his brushes with death, Jeff said he'd never leave this dangerous, beautiful place.

***

For most people who get to witness a live volcano it's a memory they never forget. The sheer power of nature is on full display. No one I met during this production had more fun volcano watching than Jimmy Hall and Stefanie Brendl.

I had seen spectacular footage of their adventures online and arranged to meet them in Hawaii. Jimmy and Stef took their sport to new heights: they paraglided over active volcanoes.

In case you don't know what a paraglider is, it's basically a rectangular parachute that catches the breeze right before you step off a cliff.

If that's not thrilling enough, these two hiked up active volcanoes then glided out over the vent. I caught up with them, where else, but at the top of a mountain. The Big Island's Mauna Kea has an elevation of 13,796 feet. To put this into perspective, I later learned that Mount Everest base camp is around 17,600 feet.

Mauna Kea is the peak that houses the world's largest observatory for optical, infrared, and sub-millimeter astronomy. Because it's so high up and in the middle of the ocean there is virtually no extraneous light. It is an excellent spot for stargazing.

The day of the interview we started at our hotel at sea level and stopped halfway up to acclimate to the altitude. Once up top, Jimmy and Stef, no strangers to altitude, bounded over the landscape with vigor. I, on the other hand, got woozy and lightheaded every time I moved my head.

Jimmy recalled for me how they had recently taken their chutes to the top of the highly active Batur Volcano on the island of Bali in Indonesia.

"You can get really good, extended high altitude flights over the Batur Volcano. We were paragliding straight over it, looking down at the volcano shooting lava up. We were walking right up to the edge and standing on the edge as it erupted. We just kept pushing it and pushing it and eventually we ended up standing on the edge when she went."

Jimmy Hall and Stefanie Brendl approaching the edge of the Batur volcano.

Their home video footage documented an enormous explosion followed by Jimmy, Stef, and a third friend racing down the slope of the volcano at breakneck speed while boulders of hot smoking rocks pounded and shattered all around them.

In the end all three were cut, bruised and bleeding, lucky to have escaped with their lives.

"Most of you are probably going 'that is really stupid,' but we got away with it - and we probably won't do it again - but we have a great story to tell," related Jimmy, smiling.

Moments after he pledged not to do it again, Jimmy invited me to paraglide with him in a tandem glider over the Stromboli Volcano in Italy that was in full eruption at the time. I was seriously debating the offer when I concluded that altitude sickness must have briefly affected my reasoning. I politely declined.

When I later told this story to friends, they usually poked me on the arm, telling me I was crazy to pass up the chance to paraglide over a volcano with a guy like Jimmy. That may have been true, but I didn't see them lining up to fly over an active volcano with him either.

A few years later, Jimmy got a big break as the host of *Shark Week* on Discovery. An avid shark diver, Jimmy wanted to dispel some of the rumors surrounding these majestic creatures.

Unfortunately, on May 9th, 2007, during a break in production, Jimmy Hall suffered a tragic accident while base jumping north of the Arctic Circle. After he and some friends had jumped off a tall ice shelf Jimmy became disoriented due to the all-white landscape and mistimed his chute opening.

The area is so remote it is only accessible by plane, snowmobile then dogsled. It took three days for rescuers to recover his body. Jimmy died doing what he loved. He once told CNN, "I'd rather blow up than rust."

Today, Stef continues the work they started together, educating the public about the true nature of sharks.

Jimmy Hall was my friend. I miss his crazy smile and try-anything attitude. He was one of a kind.

***

I have learned that friendships are important in life, maybe one of the most important things.

In Berlin, my apartment window looks down from the fourth floor onto a courtyard, a patchwork of backyards, walkways, trash cans and gardens, dominated by a large playground for children from a daycare center. Today everything is covered in a thin layer of new snow.

Now it is very quiet and there are few signs of life – a puff of steam from a distant rooftop, a lone diner sitting silently in the window of a restaurant.

I watch a magpie carry a twig and lay it at various intersections of a bare linden tree. She patently tries out different intersections of the tree before selecting a strong V-shaped space high up. With each twig she is doing what magpies do, laying the groundwork for a home, and soon, a new generation.

Each day at lunchtime the courtyard erupts with the sound of children playing. There are about twenty of them. The children all look to be around the age of three.

Looking down on the courtyard and watching the children play I think about my own life, my victories, my defeats, my childhood, my hopes and my dreams. It feels like such a long time ago.

Their lives are just beginning. All their memories still to be made. Yet, even from a distance, it seems a distinct personality has already developed in each of them.

A few sit alone, like the little girl on the swing, almost still, head down, her feet not quite touching the ground. Others seem to run endlessly. Some just sit and talk.

As children, the friends we choose are the first important choices we make. In fact, the kids we choose to hang out with – and those who choose to hang out with us – often have a meaningful impact on the rest of our lives.

Later that day, when the children have all gone, the apartment is very quiet again. I miss them.

I hope they grow up to have the chance to be whatever they want to be.

I kick off my boots. Another day has ended and I know that my time in Berlin is a gift but it will end soon and I must return to the business of life. I am thankful for the time I have had here.

I feel like I am finding my voice for the first time and I don't want it to end. But I have things to do, children to raise, jobs to complete, bills to pay and all the other things I'm taking a break from.

I pull back the drapes and look out the window at the dark courtyard below. Tired, I collapse onto the small couch and turn on the TV.

Bored quickly with the only two channels available in English, I flip open my laptop and spend the rest of the evening drinking beer while watching snippets of *Top Gear* on YouTube.

By the end of the evening I feel a kinship with Jeremy Clarkson, Richard Hammond and James May. Those guys go all over the world on great adventures. I used to do that.

***

The next leg of the journey for volcano watching would take me to Costa Rica.

I traveled with a first-rate crew, Gonzo Accame as camera operator and Tom Everly as the audio guy. These two were a great couple of guys to spend some time with. Always smiling, telling war stories from life on the road. And they had a nice chemistry working together.

They told me a story when they were on location at some Caribbean beach where they'd need to shoot under wet conditions. Tommy had an idea, an old trick to prevent the microphone from getting water damaged. "We need to find a drug store, " he said. Taking a break from production, the intrepid duo set off to find a pharmacy.

Now you've got to picture them together: Gonzo, a husky, hirsute Peruvian and Tommy, a compact, wiry little guy with glasses and a permanent smile.

They march up to the pharmacist and Gonzo asks, "We're in a hurry. We need some condoms." To which Tommy quickly added, "Unlubricated!"

I would've liked to see the expression on that pharmacist's face.

We all had a lot of road experiences but everyone would agree, Tommy told the best stories.

One night over dinner he recalled the epic tale of a videographer in China who was among a wave of journalists asked to leave during the 1989 uprising. The videographer begged his employer to let him stay in Beijing for a while. He had a hunch something big was about to happen.

His boss granted him three weeks in a hotel to follow up on his instincts. But that would be it.

The videographer set up a camera on the balcony of a hotel overlooking Tiananmen Square and solicited the help of a buddy to help watch for something, anything.

An earlier violent crackdown on the protesters by Chinese government forces led many journalists to leave the country, believing the big story was behind them. But Tommy's friend held out.

Then, on June 5th, Tank Man took his stand. The iconic footage of a lone unarmed man carrying what appeared to be bags of groceries as he stood down an approaching tank became a metaphor for a generation of frustration by the Chinses people.

The only problem, Tommy's friend was in the bathroom.

It was his buddy that captured the career-making footage. Tommy's friend emerged from the shitter only to find a hand-made sign, on which was scrawled, "Thanks for the pisser!"

In Costa Rica, we first did a few interviews in the San Jose area, the big entry city where the airport is, and then had dinner with Glory, our local contact.

She informed me of our first possible danger - kidnapping. The practice had recently become a big problem in Costa Rica and here I was getting ready to travel into remote hills with about $100,000 worth of equipment and no protection. And I thought the volcano was the biggest danger.

The next day we set out for the erupting Arenal Volcano with our guide, Jeff Otico. Otico was a transplanted American and a well-respected naturalist.

The trip to Arenal was about a four-hour drive on terrible roads. I've never been happier to have a guide. I can't imagine us trying to find the way by ourselves.

At that time, in Costa Rica, the roads had no names, the directions done by landmarks, many of which only exist in the memories of the residents, and there were precious few signs of any kind. For example, one area is called the Coca Cola district after the large bottling plant that used to be there but retains no remnant of the plant today.

I bought footage from a small Costa Rican production company and had to mail the check to 'the house by the library with the yellow shutters.'

If driving directions weren't complicating things enough, oncoming cars and trucks constantly swerved into our lane to avoid huge potholes. We were told that the national elections had just taken place and the officials often did not repair the roads in districts where their opponents had strong support. The resulting potholes were large enough to bury a man.

But as we drove, the landscape outside of San Jose became beautiful and exotic. We shot scenic footage of tropical waterfalls that roared down on us as we walked on skyways and trails through the rain forest. I saw toucans, sloths, parrots and howler monkeys in the wild.

One area had trees full of giant iguanas - some up to 5 feet long. We got right up on them. They can move quite fast, but they just stared back at us. We were close enough to touch them.

The Arenal Volcano

Soon we reached Arenal and the giant erupting volcano loomed before us. Our first big shoot involved taking a hot air balloon up as a new vantage point for volcano watching. In preparation we spent the first two nights at a remote lodge named the Tilajari Resort.

The night before the launch, we had a planning dinner with the balloonists while geckos scurried on the walls behind us. The balloonists informed me that the woman who was scheduled to fly with us - so I could have someone on-camera to interview about the experience - turned up sick. She had to be replaced.

Who could I get to fly in a balloon the next morning at dawn in the remote jungle of Costa Rica? I had no Costa Rican fixer.

The balloonist made a few harried phone calls from the bar and came up with a local teenager who was willing to fly. Whew. Crisis solved.

After dinner we set out for our cabins. The crew had a cabin facing the parking lot for easy access to the equipment but I had a cabin to myself, in the back, facing the river.

Costa Rica boasts some of the largest crocodiles in the world and I was told some have been spotted in the wild up to 20 feet long. I was told over dinner that an 18-foot crocodile had been spotted that day lurking in the river behind my cabin.

To make matters worse, my cabin was the last one in the compound, right next to the edge of the rainforest and down by the water. I was just a tad nervous heading back there alone at night. I spoke to a few of the other guests who confirmed that they had indeed seen the big croc, but so far, I hadn't. The last thing I wanted was for the croc to see me first. They are extremely fast over short distances. And was it dark that night - pitch black except for my trusty flashlight.

I nearly leapt out of my skin when a 4-foot iguana crossed the path right in front of me and waddled into the woods, but I thankfully saw no sign of the big croc.

At about 4:00 AM the following morning we got up and set out into the night for the balloon launch. We drove to a fog-shrouded field and began to spread out the huge, colorful hot air balloon. As we pulled the basket from the back of the pick-up truck, the pilot told me to be careful where I step. "This field is snake-infested," he said. "They like to eat the rats," his helper said, looking around cautiously.

I didn't know if they were pulling my leg or not, but I watched where I stepped.

I was told that the balloonists had never launched from this spot before but chose it so we could get the best possible look at the volcano from the balloon.

By daybreak, the weather was still quite foggy but the balloonists thought it might be clear above the clouds. We inflated the balloon with the pilot, our teenager and the crew in the basket and launched them up.

I shot the ascent from the ground with my camera. After take-off, the balloon silently disappeared into the low clouds. No one could have predicted what would happen next.

Here's how it was relayed to me by Gonzo.

"We slid into the clouds and couldn't see a thing. Next, we caught a very strong sideways wind that blew the balloon so hard the basket swung out violently behind it. Then the whole balloon started to shake hard.

"I looked at the pilot. As long as he was cool, I was cool. It was really scary for a bit. Then, finally, we popped out of the top of the clouds and the balloon settled down a little. We couldn't see the volcano, just miles and miles of fluffy clouds beneath us.

"Our teenage girl clung onto the side of the basket. As it turned out, it was her first time flying. She'd never even been in a plane.

"Then the pilot took a GPS reading. That's when he said, 'Uh Oh - we're heading fifty kilometers per hour… straight for the volcano.'"

Meanwhile Tommy, the audio guy, was sitting on the floor of the basket. He had to duck down to stay out of Gonzo's shot. It was even more terrifying for Tommy, because he couldn't see what was going on.

"All I could see was out of the two little holes on the side of the basket. I saw the ground zipping away and everything below getting real small, real fast. Then the whole thing started to shake. Man, it was wild!"

After the balloon disappeared into the clouds, I had no idea what was going on. I was on the ground in the chase vehicle. The owner of the balloon company was driving. She could communicate with the pilot by radio and when she heard the pilot's heading, she ordered them to come down as fast as possible.

We couldn't see them but we also had a GPS device tracking them. Sure enough, they were heading straight for the volcano.

The winds around Arenal are notoriously unpredictable. Locked between the Pacific Ocean and the Caribbean Sea, it is influenced by the weather of both. And the heat from the volcanic activity helps the volcano generate its own weather patterns.

This particular morning, the entire mountain was shrouded in fog and we couldn't see the volcano at all. But we knew they were very, very close.

The balloon emerged from the clouds a little northwest of Fortuna, the small town at the base of the volcano. While descending the pilot told the crew and the teenager to bend their legs and prepare to hit hard. They did come down hard, crash-landing in a tall sugar cane field. The sugar cane made for a rough, brittle landing.

The first bounce toppled the crew and bounced them around in the basket, but the second hit really nailed them, ripping the 30-pound camera from Gonzo's shoulder. He barely held on, catching it with his fingertips. After being dragged through the tall, brittle sugar cane, the basket finally came to rest surrounded by 8-foot-high cane.

The owner and I had to take down a barbed-wire fence and hack in with machetes to get them out.

Soon local farmers and children gathered to watch. After twenty minutes hacking through the high brush, I first saw Tommy who exclaimed, "Dr. Livingston, I presume!"

The seasoned pilot confided afterwards that it was the most frightening experience he'd ever had ballooning. They were all shaken up but thankfully everyone was alright.

Later that day, we drove back to the spot where the balloon had landed. By this time the fog had lifted and the skies were clear. We looked up and realized just how close they'd come. We were literally at the base of one of the world's most active volcanoes. Tommy recalled, "Once I saw where we were and realized where we landed, I was really shaken up. I had no idea we'd come that close."

But we hadn't gotten the shots needed. We needed footage of the volcano from the balloon. Reluctantly I told the crew that, the next morning, they'd have to try again.

That night I replaced the shaken local teenager with another young woman.

Jamie was the daughter of the hotel owner and had just returned to town that afternoon. Jamie was beautiful and eloquent, with a strong command of English and a great, daring spirit. And, thankfully for our frazzled crew, the next morning things seemed to go well right from the start.

This time we decided to launch from a spot more familiar to the balloon crew. The pre-dawn weather was hazy but nothing like the thick fog we'd experienced the day before.

As the sun rose, the haze burned off to reveal horses in the distant pasture and good visibility. The balloon gracefully ascended into the light clouds. "The silence was mesmerizing and the flight was very smooth," said Tommy. "The clouds even had a soft scent I can't describe. It was beautiful."

This time they could see the volcano looming in the distance. The footage was great and Jamie took direction well. And she looked comfortable in the balloon. What a contrast to the day before. They could see the volcano, it was a beautiful flight and it made a great segment for the program.

Even the pilot smiled as they slowly descended among the top of the rainforest trees. There, they were treated to a birds-eye view of monkeys and toucans.

The balloon gracefully landed in a field where we gave local children a free tethered ride in the warm morning sun. And when the camera crew wanted a shot of the balloon landing, I even went up for a quick flight.

I felt bad about having to send them back up and Gonzo later confided that he would not have flown the second time if he didn't have to. Everyone was pretty shaken by the crash landing. But all admitted that the second flight was flawless and it turned out to be a great shot and a perfect day.

I had received a tip that a local restaurant owner had shot some good footage the last time the volcano had a big eruption. I set up a meeting with him, a man known to us as Don Luis.

We were told by the balloon operator that the custom was to be very reverential to Don Luis, to treat him with respect, have dinner with him in his restaurant, discuss anything but business at the meal then, only when the meal was over, ask to see his volcano footage.

I've learned that, unlike in America, in many parts of the world it is considered bad form to discuss business over a meal. I've grown to embrace that, too.

We arrived at the restaurant in the middle of the afternoon. In contrast to the bright sunshine outside, we entered a very dark restaurant. The shades were drawn shut and only a soft beam of sunlight sliced across a huge dark wooden table. At the head of the table sat Don Luis.

I was introduced to him like he was some head of state. He reached out his hand and clasped mine. He spoke very little English and I spoke very little Spanish but fortunately Gonzo, who grew up in Peru, was fluent in both and acted as interpreter.

As the producer and de facto head of my delegation I was expected to discuss things with the Don. After a nice meal we got down to business.

Don Luis had what he described as fantastic, incredible footage on his camcorder. He only had the original tape and no copies were ever created. To make matters worse, the tape was in an old format, and it would be very difficult to find a tape deck that would play it back.

There was a small camera shop in town but Don Luis forbade us from going anywhere near the shop since he didn't trust the owner and thought the guy might steal his precious footage.

I proposed to Don Luis that he lend us both his tape and his camera so we could play back the tape with his camera and transfer the footage to our own tape deck. He was very cautious and thought about it.

After a while, Don Luis said he trusted me but he also threatened that if I stole his tape and camera he would track me down and make me very sorry. It made me recall Greek customs and the threat I received from the assistant director. Only this scene also threw in a little sinister ambiance from *The Godfather*.

I offered a generous compensation to him and told him we'd pay half now and half upon return of the camera and tape. I also pledged to take good care of his stuff. Don Luis agreed and signed a document I had drafted giving us the rights to his footage. We shook hands again and the crew and I left.

I treated his camera like the Presidential football. I asked Tommy to do the transfer that same night. Don Luis was right, the footage was spectacular.

The next day I promptly returned the tape and camera to him, paid him the balance, complemented him again on the fine meal we shared and left feeling like I had spent some time in a real-life crime novel.

Tired and trying to think ahead, I decided to remain at the hotel and make some phone calls to set up our next adventure while the crew and our guide went into the jungle to get a few shots of some of the local wildlife.

In the woods, Otico spotted this disgusting creature – a turkey vulture - in the dense brush and the crew went after it. Gonzo chased it around with the camera and I was told got the bird pretty worked up. The bird got all puffy and started hacking at the crew.

Then Otico spotted its nest, complete with a few little eggs. In the turmoil of the chase, Tommy wound up between the bird and the nest, so the bird started to attack him. Tommy froze as the bird approached, hacking and wheezing in his direction.

"Careful," Otico offered, "they tend to vomit on their enemies. It's pretty vile stuff."

That's all Tommy needed to hear. The last thing he wanted was to carry the essence of turkey vomit with him for the next few days.

Meanwhile, hoping to get the bird to vomit on Tommy, Gonzo continued to antagonize the bird with the camera and gave chase again.

As Gonzo slogged through the muddy underbrush, batting away tree branches, Otico also cautioned him, "Watch out for the eyelash vipers in there. They are tiny snakes that live in branches about eye level. They're poisonous and extremely dangerous."

Now it was Gonzo's turn to freeze. Fortunately, I was happy to learn they all emerged from the jungle without any poison or vomit. And I was glad I stayed back at the hotel.

Our next stop was at the Tabacon Resort for a few nights. Tabacon lies in a valley at the base of Arenal Volcano and is among the finest luxury hotels in all of Costa Rica. It truly was beautiful, but it was literally at the base of the volcano and had been evacuated at least three times recently due to volcanic activity.

Here we were, eating and sleeping right at the base of the volcano.

Tabacon was built on the ruins of the town that was destroyed by the Arenal Volcano in 1968. Scientists have warned about the danger here for years and predict that one day Tabacon will again be engulfed in a deadly pyroclastic flow. It only exists because of the dozen or so hot springs and the luxury resort that supports them.

Signs everywhere indicate the danger: "Do not venture beyond this point" and "Evacuation Route" postings were common.

The real reason the resort exists is because Tabacon is a real money-maker in a relatively poor country. Everyone we spoke to understood the imminent danger but no one would discuss it on camera for fear of losing their job. I understood the possibilities, too. I only hoped they wouldn't manifest themselves during our brief visit.

To make the danger even more mysterious, the top of the volcano was often obscured by clouds. We could see the base from our rooms but the top was always shrouded. We could hear activity and eruptions flowing down the other side of the mountain but couldn't see anything.

One morning while Tommy slept in, Gonzo and I were on the verandah enjoying a cup of coffee. It was about 6:30 AM when we heard *BOOM BOOM BOOM!* We looked at each other.

"That was the volcano erupting," we both said at the same time.

I looked down to see concentric circles in my coffee cup. The only other time I'd seen that was during a mild earthquake in Los Angeles. In case there was any doubt, this confirmed that we were indeed sitting at the base of one of the world's most active volcanoes.

We just sat there silently, holding the warm coffee mugs in our hands, wondering at the sheer power of nature. It was a feeling I'll never forget.

Later that day we drove around the far side of the volcano to El Silencio to see if we could spot any lava on the slopes. Sure enough, I saw huge boulders of red lava careening down the side of the volcano. They were trailing dust behind them as they burst on the rocks below.

"I can stop chasing volcanoes now," I thought. "I've seen a good one."

We planned to interview Otico there, but the weather changed quickly. The rain moved in and the volcano was obscured once again.

That evening after dinner, Tommy and I headed to the famous Tabacon Springs to check them out. The springs are a series of pools and waterfalls connected by a very warm, free-flowing river. The water is between 98 and 120 degrees Fahrenheit.

It was a very strange feeling, sitting under a hot waterfall, in full knowledge that the water was heated by the active volcano behind me. I even took a turn on the hot waterslide down to the swim-up bar.

It's a fun place to visit. No wonder the authorities are reluctant to close it. But the whole time I was in the area I felt like I was tempting fate.

Each night I was in Tabacon I slept in my clothes and kept my shoes in the same place by the bed so I could slip into them quickly in the dark in case of an emergency evacuation. I had purchased a small red light at the Hawaiian observatories like the one stargazers use to mark remote telescopes and clipped it to my bag so I could locate it by the door if I needed to flee in the middle of the night. I even practiced leaping out of bed, into my shoes and running out the door.

Then one night I was reading in bed when *BOOM!* I heard an explosion and the room plunged into total darkness.

As practiced, I sprang from the bed, slipped into my shoes, grabbed my bag and ran into the parking lot. I stood there, frantically looking from left to right. I was ready to bolt full-speed out of the parking lot and into the road when I realized I was completely alone.

It turned out it the culprit was only a brief power failure. I felt like a fool but fortunately no one was around to witness it.

I slunk back to my room - but I still readied my bag and shoes for the next time.

While at Tabacon we were slated to interview Jan Beers, manager of the Canopy Tour. A canopy tour sends participants zooming high through the treetops on zip lines. It's a fun adventure and you can see the volcano from the platforms high in the trees.

Otico, Gonzo and me, preparing for the zip line.

To get some interesting footage, and to have a little fun, I suggested to the crew that we check out the Canopy Tour by joining up with the next group that was going. Gonzo, Tommy, Otico and I reported to the office where we signed waivers and were outfitted with gear, then we marched up the hill to the first platform.

We needed to climb a tall rope ladder to get to the launch site, and Gonzo was so scared, I wasn't sure he was going to make it. He really wanted to turn around, but he knew Tommy and I would rag on him for the rest of the trip.

Since Tommy was still looking for revenge after Gonzo chased the vomiting turkey vulture towards him, he pressed Gonzo and Gonzo pressed on.

Gonzo's eyes coming up the ladder behind me were as big as saucers as he slowly pulled up one step at a time and joined us at the top. He was so scared that he was shaking the whole platform, which was only about half the size of a small coffee table and so high up in the trees that you couldn't see the ground, only the tops of the trees below.

Once we were up there, we took turns as experienced guides strapped our harness to a pulley and we zipped from one tree to another, each perhaps forty yards away.

The idea is to freefall on an inclined cable toward the next platform. When you get close to the end, you apply the "brake" by pulling down on the top of the cable with your gloved hand, thereby slowing your descent. Gonzo misinterpreted the guide's signal and hit the brake too soon, finding himself dangling high above the trees, ten feet short of the next platform. I'd never seen the big man move so fast as he turned himself around and pulled that cable, hand over hand, for the final few feet. Upon reaching the platform, he hugged the tree before rappelling down to the next launch platform.

We could see the volcano looming in the distance and I knew it would make a fun segment for the program. We continued the tour, zipping along the treetops and getting footage for the show with our mini DV cameras until we reached the last platform.

The last zip of the canopy tour was the wildest - from the top of a cliff. We had to zip down, approximately 250 feet on a 45-degree angle to poolside and the end of the tour. It was the only way down, and Gonzo was the happiest man in the world when, with a little help from gravity, he landed safely on the ground.

The interview with Jan went well and soon we were heading back to San Jose.

We still needed to interview Otico, but the rain was rolling back in. We decided to drive out of the weather and find a quiet spot somewhere on the trip back. About an hour out of San Jose we turned off the Pan American Highway and looked for a location for our interview. We headed down a remote road toward what we thought might be a vista of the valley. Soon the pavement ended, and we were way back in the wild hills of Costa Rica.

We pressed further down the dirt road, over more hills and past some houses, to a very remote area. Then the road turned sharply up a hill and we suddenly dead-ended in front of a shack so weather-beaten it seemed to be standing by the grace of a single rusty nail.

Out popped a farmer who waved to us. We stopped the engine and realized that the place was dead silent, perfect for an interview. The old shack even had a rustic old banana plantation sign above the door, straight out of set design school.

We asked the farmer if we could shoot in front of his shack and he loved the idea - with the caveat that we all take a brief tour of his farm when we finished.

The interview with Otico went well until the farmer's rooster started crowing. By then we'd had enough, gave up on the interview, met the farmer's dad and took a little tour. The guy was so proud of his farm and so happy to host our brief visit. Gonzo even gave the farmer his Travel Channel hat and the guy beamed. I have a feeling he proudly wore that hat a long time.

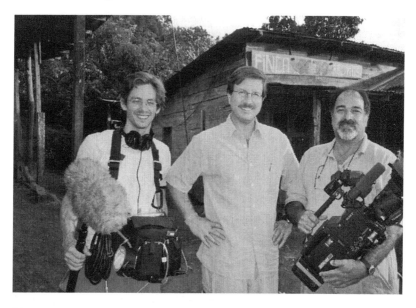

Tommy, me and Gonzo in Costa Rica shooting *Best Place to Watch a Volcano* at the farmer's ranch in the remote hills. Note the rustic sign over the door. The crew is smiling because this was the last day of the trip and they knew I couldn't ask them to go up in another hot air balloon or face another zip line.

Thankfully I returned home and wasn't kidnapped.

Upon my return to the office I began to assemble the show with my editor, Rob Deege and my associate producer, Shaun Gildea. I had shot or collected enough footage to do two hours instead of just one so I went back to the network and offered them a two-hour special. They loved the idea.

Craig Sechler did a great voiceover, Jeff Order did another magnificent original score, Jim Ferrara cut the final master and Eric Van Ryzin helped with some additional local shooting. Special thanks go to Cathryn Garland for her guidance and Lori Rothschild for her constant support and encouragement.

But Mark Edmondson really made the volcano show burst from the screen with his post production audio mix. I know he worked hard on it, adding sound effects, making the audio sound better through enhancements and noise reduction.

The title sequence alone had something like eighteen additional sound effects such as the sound of bullets whizzing by under the flying lava rocks and the sound of creaking bending ship metal under the building stress of the erupting volcano. He really worked hard to make this show come alive.

Mark even came in on the weekend to finish up. On one of the Saturdays, after getting caught in a torrential downpour, Mark mixed the show in his underwear while his clothes dried. Now that's dedication.

After the show was cut and delivered, Cathryn Garland, my executive producer, said, "Love the show. But cut the title sequence."

Oh well. That's show biz. My elaborate title sequence never aired in the US. But I did manage to keep it on the international version of the show which was seen around the world in 35 countries.

As far as I know, *Best Place to Watch a Volcano* was Discovery Communications first totally internal-produced program.

The show debuted on the Travel Channel in June 2002 and was a hit. Entertainment Weekly put it in their *What to Watch* column and People Magazine made it a *Pick of the Week*. Fifty NBC-affiliated stations across the nation picked up the story of the wedding on the lava flow, each with the Travel Channel plug. The network was thrilled with my program.

After I delivered the final show to the network I collapsed into the chair at my desk. It hit me all at once.

I realized that I had done it.

I reached my mountaintop.

I had gotten all my questions answered. I had met my goal, the one I envisioned so long ago sitting on that owl.

Knowing full well that you must celebrate your victories in life I threw a big premier party with co-workers, family and friends. That was a good time.

The only problem I had was that, after a long journey, I had found myself on top of my personal mountain and when you are on the mountaintop, looking around, you realize there is nowhere to go but down.

But for me, that was OK. My life had changed in the years between sitting on my parent's couch dreaming of making a documentary and the day I accomplished it. I had done all I wanted to do in network television.

I recalled the time I heard some old men talking. None of them wished they could've spent more time at the office. To a man they all regretted they didn't spend more time with their kids when they were young.

My children were still small and I left the chaotic world of network television to spend more time with them, to raise them. And that's what I did.

Fortunately, I was able to return to a simpler job, a place with regular hours, limited travel, good benefits, nice people and very little stress.

I had a lot of friends that had a much harder time after leaving Discovery. Not all, but some. Those few identified themselves as that powerful figure from that well-known company. And when it was all over they didn't know how to identify themselves any more.

I always consciously avoided identifying myself as that powerful person from the famous place so when it ended I knew who I was. I tried to be the same guy all along.

I learned that from professional athletes. The best ones know that when they're hot they're never as good as their fans think they are. And when they're not, they're never as bad as their fans think they are either. But for many, it's really hard to walk away from a big stage.

Curtis Martin said at his induction into the Pro Football Hall of Fame, "Out of all the things that I have achieved, one of the things that I've learned is that it's not necessarily what you achieve in life that matters most, but it's who you become in the process of those achievements."

I couldn't agree more.

And from the day I found my mountaintop, no matter where I went or what I did, the words of another legendary NFL figure, coach Bill Parcells, would echo in my mind. "For the rest of your life, nobody could ever tell you that you couldn't do it."

AUTHOR'S NOTE

My life has changed significantly since the time where this story ends. I have worked hard, faced challenges, raised my children, loved deeply and lost profoundly. But real love is never a waste of time.

One of the people I lost along the way was a dear friend and mentor, Cicily Janus. She helped me out immeasurably with this book. Cicily Janus passed away from cancer at the age of 39. She left behind three beautiful daughters.

I was inspired by Cicily.

Late in the summer of 2016 I knew she was going to die soon and I asked if I could visit. In September I flew to Colorado and spent five days with her. During my daily visits we talked, even managed to laugh. She was quite weak but still lucid.

Each day driving to hospice I had a magnificent view of the Rockies. In the morning they were backlit by a brilliant blue, in the evening dancing under shades of red and pink, at night black ghosts above the twinkling lights. She was surrounded by all that strength and durability but the mountains couldn't give her any of it.

She told me of her favorite hikes and I managed to take in three of them, showing her the videos from my phone. That made her happy. We both knew she'd never get to see those places again.

I met some of Cicily's friends - very fine people - and she made sure to make them my friends as well. Always connecting people, even up to the end.

While we sat and talked, she spoke a lot about her children and showed me the journals she'd written – three of them – one for each girl. Words for the day of their wedding, the day they give birth, the day they graduate college and all the other special occasions she could think of but would never live to see.

Late in my trip I gave Cicily some of this book to critique. She'd been working on it, off and on, along with me for many years. For a short while it gave her purpose, something she desperately wanted as her body slowly failed her. She encouraged me to write in my own voice. So, if some of the passages here were spicy, it's because of that chat.

That afternoon, all Cicily's vast knowledge came pouring out, rapid fire. Her mind was sharp as she cut through the haze of disease and drugs. She was alive and connected again. It was beautiful. But we both knew it couldn't last.

On the last day of my visit I asked her what she'd learned during her lifetime. She didn't hesitate.

"Love. It's the only thing that matters," she said.

When it came time to go I wanted to leave her a gift. But what?

I decided to sing her a song and we both cried a little. Wiping away the tears I reached into my bag and pulled out a t-shirt I'd spotted in a thrift shop. Probably worn by a camp counselor on the last day of summer it read, "It's not goodbye, just goodbye for now."

Cicily laughed when she opened it and draped it over her hospital gown, primping like a model. Then I gave her a kiss, took her head in my hands, looked into her eyes and said, "it's not goodbye, just goodbye for now."

Cicily passed away peacefully not too long after my visit. The world will miss her. So will I.

I wrote this book over the course of at least ten years. I did two major revisions, each in Berlin, and that wonderful, vibrant city became a part of the book. It was the place where I reflected on my career once again, the thread that tied it together.

Today, Berlin is the greatest little secret in the world. I hope it never changes.

I hope you enjoyed my story. And I hope you can stand on the peak of your own mountaintop one day.

Don't let anybody tell you that you can't do it.

ACKNOWLEDGEMENTS

I would like to thank the real-life people mentioned in this book for helping me along the way and accepting me as one of their own. They are all fine, decent and hard-working people. I recognize that their memories of the events described in this book may be different than my own. The book was not intended to hurt anyone and I regret in advance any unintentional harm resulting from the publishing and marketing of this memoir.

I'd also like to offer a special thanks to the following people who helped me on my journey.

There is a belief that everyone knows someone who has been in a film with Kevin Bacon, separated by no more than six degrees. I was an extra in Barry Levinson's film *Diner*, along with the actor Kevin Bacon, so I'm one degree. The following people are only two degrees.

If you know any of them, you're only three degrees… and so on.

Here they are, in no particular order. Thank you all.

Martin Pearson, Nathan Antila, Greg Letourneau, Paisley Graham, Bobby Hird, Ingrid Floyd, Mary Ellen Iwata, Rick Gambo, Dave Shapiro, Pete Diorio, Cat Najarian, Arthur Forrest, Harun Guler, Ed Neenan, Kim Hirose, Rachel McAtee Schaffer, Stacy Goldstein, Jay Schneider, Tam Anderson, Aaron Garnett, Bob Ligouri, Alex Katis, Ray Kreiner, Larry Bowers, Dave Vergauwen, Colleen Carter, Anne Goetz, Lori Link, Tom Pokorny, Alisha Simms, Amanda Diddlemeyer, John Fant, Ali Felix, Amy Barton, Anita Darnell, Mick and Ann Kalber, Brooks Moore, Anna Hansen, Dave Emmons, Keith Nelson, Virginia Nicolaidis, Mattie Miles, Sergio Villafane, Arturo & Helen, Danny Salerno, Beth Nardone, Jimmy Swierczewski,

Charles MacCormick, Anthony Bogdan, Bob Ferrier, Bob Sitrick, Steve Burns, Cicily Janus, Joni Campbell, John MacKerron, Dick Ochs, Jeff Kidwell, Darlene Blevins, Melissa Hilbish, Kathy Sirota, Jeannie Howe, Britt Sjoerdsma, Heather Norris, Chuck Dutrow, Kevin Fuscus, Thomas Cutler, Kat, Diane Burns, Dave Dunham, Dave Henn, David "Dude" Plourde, Diana Engle, Azat Safavi, Ardis Cohen, Anatole, Don Wehner, Leigh Sutherland, Peggy Benner, Caryn Sorosky Weaver, Dan Alvarez, Don Thoms, Duane Samuda, Elizabeth Miller, Eric Van Ryzin, Ed Colbert, Erika Goldthwaite, Vance Welch, Laura Childs, Steve Curran, Tom Goertel, Annie Laboda, Mary Clare Helldorfer, Susie Miles, Russ Vollmers, Keith Nadeau, Bob Hamlin, Vicki Cristiano, Gaynelle Evans, Gena McCarthy, Gonzo Accame, Heather Moran, Ingrid Gorman, Mark Finkelpearl, Jim Ferrara, Mark Griffin, Pam Whyte, Jacqui De Phillips, Jeff Order, Jesse Gordon, Jim Kowats, Jim Lefter, Jodi Anderson, Sarah Beechy, Jody Roesler, John Cosense, Jojo, John Dockman, John Lowry, Karen Kraft, David Kraft, Joni Lescher, Julie House, Julie Nadezna, Margo, Kandy Collins, Quinn Collins, Kim Hirose, Laurie Altland, Steve Cook, Jay Harrison, Frank Ayd, Billy Ezell, Leslie Ralston-Rakow, Lisa Marber-Rich, Lori Rothschild, Marc Kohn, Mark Kozaki, Marlene Tolosa-Fairbrother, Lynda Bender, Steve Peters, Bill Peterson, Bill Fleming, Lorraine Imwold, Carl Arnold, Tom Sprankle, Debbie, Klapaska, Lyle Hein, Brian Wade, Dale Drenner, Chuck Hoffman, Maureen Leypoldt, Mike Fevang, Mike Shive, Mike English, Mike Quattrone, Nancy Lavin, John Brann, John Capobianco, Ron Riddle, Eeva Reetta Laiho, Terri Askew, Neale Smith, Diane DeMarco, Pamela Deutsch, Paul Markey, Mark Edmondson, Renee Beck, Rob Deege, Russ Harris, Sean Burke, Donna Hilton, Wes Konick, Jim Burger, Jo Ann Burton, Deirdre Butcher, Deborah Rudicille, Sharon Gillooly, Kevin Estis, Monique Lyons, Eileen O'Neill, Shaun Gildea, Kim Blair, Denise Buchman, Christina Duvall, James McCrae, John Johnson, Stephanie Bosco, Steve Cheskin, Tom Everly, Quentin Eyers, Theo Smith, Tim Brown, Tricia Steadman Jump, Will Lyman, William Beck, Jamie

Roberts, Mary Ellen Iwata, Mike Pianowski, Serge, Susan Ottradovic, Thunder, Mark Kozaki, Stacey DiLorenzo, Jeff Atkinson, Marilyn Beery, Rafael Alvarez, Wayne Highland, Mike Bogasky, Laura Rodriguez, Bob White, Laura Thomson, Alex Ross, Paula Ehrmann, Matt Moran, Jeff Atkinson, Dave Taschler, Gunnar Molen, Amy Zavadil, Marly Carpenter, Thea Golden, Monika Cebulla, Patricia Poljak, Rebecca McCullough, John Cosenze, Leanne Norton Long, Chuck Leimbach, Jeff Krulik, Tom Fritschi, Gregg Landry, Ann Lovelace, Chris Fetner, Karen Mitchell, Jamie Roberts, Juanita Ignacio, Chad Heupel, Lisa Feit, Jeff Strong, John Fletcher, Adam Eisenberg, AnnMarie Gervasio, John Reesch, Dave Shapiro, Richard Wells, Stacey DiLorenzo, Shane Ritchie, Tomi Landis and Robert Russo.

You've been mentors, co-workers, inspirations, friends, teachers and confidants. I'm grateful that our paths have crossed.

If I missed your name, forgive me. The next beer is on me.

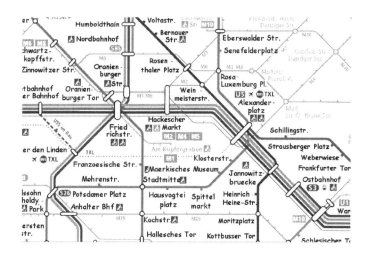

My Berlin neighborhood

ABOUT THE AUTHOR

Jeff Dugan began his career as an ashtray holder. He went on to make his mark as a documentary producer, creating original programs like *Best Place To Watch A Volcano* and *Narrow Escapes* for the Discovery Channel family of networks.

He now writes and makes small films for fun in his hometown of Baltimore.

JEFF DUGAN

Made in the USA
Middletown, DE
30 January 2018